ISBN 978-0-692-76313-1

Published by
Jostens, Inc.
3601 Minnesota Drive, #400
Minneapolis, MN 55435

JostensRenaissance.com

Contents

Introduction

Years ago I attended my first Jostens Renaissance National Conference. At the end of that conference, I sat with a notebook full of ideas and an energy for school that was unlike anything I had felt before. I could not wait to get back to school and implement the new ideas to energize my school's climate and culture. When I returned to school, I quickly learned that each idea I got needed to be altered in some way in order for it to work right for my school.

The following year I attended the Jostens Renaissance National Conference again, and I heard even more ideas. I started to think that not every idea was right for my school. I started to tune out the ideas that weren't designed exactly for my age level or demographic. At the end of the conference I had half the ideas I had the year before. I figured, this will not do. There are so many ideas out there. Why not find out as many as possible and make the adjustment to make it work with my school? That is when I decided to start collecting ideas.

The ideas that I collected are from years of visiting schools and attending the Jostens Renaissance National Conference. Many of the ideas started as something completely different, then I altered them to fit my school. Sometimes, I never implemented the idea, but it sparked a new idea that did work. For the next 16 years, I grabbed as many ideas as possible and put them into a presentation and now this book.

As you read the ideas, keep in mind that every idea may not work with your school. It may be for the wrong age level or demographic. You may use the idea as it is or change it to fit you. The goal is to spark something in you to make the idea come alive for your school. This book may have 99 ideas written, but my hope is that 10,000 new ideas are created because of the ideas I have shared.

3

I will start with sharing one idea that is guaranteed to have an impact on the climate and culture of your school: get involved with Jostens Renaissance. Renaissance is comprised of passionate educators and students from all across North America and provides ideas and resources that are proven to make a positive difference in the climate and culture of your school. Whether it's by attending a National Conference or using the resources on JostensRenaissance.com, you are certain to be inspired, motivated, and enlightened about renewing school climate and culture.

Thank you and enjoy!

Steven A. Bollar

Acknowledgements

One of the few "rules" of participating in the Renaissance community is that everyone is welcome to beg, borrow and steal ideas from each other. This means that at any Renaissance gathering, you may be chatting with another educator who says "I got this great idea last year to have my students build an XYZ" and it turns out that was actually your idea, and it passed through two other schools before landing at the current one in a completely different form. Renaissance educators take pride in contributing to the community.

That said, we wanted to acknowledge several schools, organizations and individuals whose ideas were used in this book.

Aberdeen High School
Burlington County Institute of Technology (BCIT)
Chris Dziczek
Conway High School East
Dwight Carter
Hartford School
Melanie Lindsey
NAESP Principal Communicator Newsletter, November 2012
North Hall
Penn Jersey Renaissance Collaborative
Tina Dietrich at Fountain Woods School
Tracy Mossburger

We invite all educators to share great ideas with others by submitting them to the Idea Exchange at www.JostensRenaissance.com.

Thank you to the Jostens Renaissance team, especially to Alanna Walen for her help in making this book come to life.

Finally, a special thank you to my family for putting up with my obsession.

Take It From Me: Educational Conference Overload

I recently attended the Jostens Renaissance National Conference in sunny Orlando, FL. The event was amazing. The conversation was rich, the dialog was meaningful, and the ideas were cutting edge. It was so empowering to hear about the amazing things that can be done in education focused on school culture and climate. Talking about what learning is about humbled me to the power educators hold.

During one of the sessions I presented, one of my fellow educators posed the question, "How do we return to school and relay all that we have experienced over the past few days?" He used a vacation scenario to express his concern. He outlined that the Jostens Renaissance National Conference was like an amazing vacation where he experienced incredible life changing events. He understands that he wants to share these events with his family back at school, but how should he do that without looking like he is simply sharing a slide show of his vacation? Standing in front of his school and talking about all the wonderful things that took place will fall on deaf ears. Basically, what is the next step?

It is true that others who have not experienced what you have experienced will not "get it." It becomes very frustrating and even hopeless that any meaningful change will take place. I started to think of what educators can do to start the process of implementing what they have heard at a powerful training, conference, or event. Below is the advice I gave:

Organize Your Stuff: At the end of a conference, usually your mind is blown. You have pages and pages of ideas, quotes, thoughts, names, contacts, and next-step actions. When you start to think and look at what you have, you start to feel overwhelmed with the plethora of information. Start by organizing what you have. Make three columns. Title each column, "Do Now," "Do With Help," or "Do Later With Help." It is up to you how you title your columns as long as they provide some kind of timeline. Start categorizing everything you can think of from the conference into one of the columns. As you are organizing your thoughts, more thoughts will jump into your head. Place those thoughts in one of the columns as well. Once you are done organizing, you should start to see what is doable and what needs to be done later.

Pick a Nugget: Look at everything in your "Do Now" column. Pick just one idea or "nugget" that can be implemented rather quickly and easily. If you were to pick that one nugget without organizing your ideas, you may not pick the right one. You may end up picking a nugget that is connected to several other nuggets and turn into something much bigger than it needs to be. Specifically, try to find a nugget that can be seen by many, but does not require the work of many. This will give you the most bang for your buck. You have a better chance of pulling others in once they see the simplicity of your actions and how meaningful they can be.

Presentation is Everything: Most schools require you to present to the staff or team what you experienced at your conference. As the educator said during the last session at the Jostens Renaissance National Conference, "I don't want it to feel like I am showing slides from my vacation." The way you avoid that is to tell a story and highlight your "nugget." People connect with stories. Start by sharing a story of why you need to implement your nugget. Don't start by saying what the nugget is. Simply start with the story. If your story involves students, it is even better. After telling the story, follow by giving a brief description of the conference and explain your nugget. Then sit down.

Boom! You have their hearts. You have their minds. You have them wanting more. Those who were touched and want to join in with your nugget will seek you out. You have just started a movement. Now you can share the rest of your slides from your vacation to those who want to see it.

After a great event like the Jostens Renaissance National Conference you are pumped up with ideas and feel empowered to share your enthusiasm. Unfortunately, the euphoric feeling quickly fades as you return to reality. Nevertheless, you are compelled to share your experience with others. Through this process, you will start to make a difference. You will organize the many ideas in order to find what is doable. Find the nugget that will give you the most bang for your buck. Then blow their minds with a presentation that touches the heart.

Student Engagement

100% Homework
Turn It In for a Chance to Win

Recognize students who consistently turn in their homework. At the end of each week, place the names of the students who completed 100% of their homework into a bin. Pull the name and give the student a gift certificate to the school store or snack line. If you want to ramp it up, connect with a local business to provide a special gift certificate for the 100% homework kid. Provide the business with a certificate to place in the window showing how they support the school. A local pizza place would be perfect. The entire family can enjoy a pizza dinner because the student did his/her best with homework.

Applause
Who Doesn't Love Being Greeted with Cheers?

This idea will completely confuse your students and make them smile. As the students arrive at school for the first day, have all available staff make a line at the entrance of the school. As the students enter the school, the staff applauds and cheers. The students will be shocked! They will also have a huge smile. What a great way for the students to experience the first day of school. Not only will the students feel great, so will the staff. The staff will feel even better than the students. What educator doesn't like encouraging and empowering students? This idea is easy, free, and powerful.

Best Seat in the House
Enjoy the Game in Comfort and Style

Reserve the best seats at an upcoming sporting event. If you are able to place a couch or comfy seat there, that's even better. Throughout the week, give students an opportunity to have their name placed in a drawing, for a reason established by the school. It could be for attendance, homework completion, or grades. On the day of the event, pull the name of the student. The student gets to sit in the seat with three friends or family members, and gains free entrance into the event.

Other options:
- Take a photo of each winner in the seat and post in the school and/or on social media.
- The winner gets play money to use at the concession stand.
- Announce the winner at the game and why he/she won.
- Send out a press release.
- Interview the winner for the school paper or television station.

Blaze of Glory: A Cure for Senioritis
Don't Give Up on the Seniors

Blaze of Glory is an attempt to "cure senioritis" – in other words, stop our seniors from crashing and burning academically in their final year. It is not enough that the curriculum in both English and Social Science is rigorous; the seniors need something else to keep them motivated in their final year.

Blaze of Glory is a subsection of our Jostens Renaissance program and it is exclusively for seniors. The Renaissance program seemed to no longer act as a strong incentive for seniors after semester one – we needed something more. Blaze of Glory became that something. Blaze of Glory celebrates homework completion, attendance and academic improvement at each quarter and sometimes in between.

There are a number of different incentives offered:

- **Dragon Hall of Fame – Most Improved:** The two students who make the biggest improvement in their GPA (from freshman to senior semester) and in standardized test scores are inducted into the Dragon Hall of Fame. Inductees receive a medallion at Senior Awards Night that sets them apart at graduation.

- **Senior Awards Night:** All seniors who increase their GPA by .5 or higher during their senior year are rewarded at Senior Awards Night with a badge of honor to be worn on their stole at graduation. Seniors who maintain a 3.0 or higher GPA through both semesters will also be recognized with a badge of honor to be worn on the stole at graduation.

- **Quarterly Celebrations:** Blaze of Glory holds a celebration for seniors who have improved their GPA by .5 or more from one quarter to the next. For many seniors, the 18 weeks from semester to semester is too long – they need a pat on the back at the 9-week mark, and our Blaze of Glory Quarterly Celebration accomplishes just that.

- **Monthly celebrations:** Blaze of Glory chooses a focus area each month and offers some kind of incentive. Some months are for attendance so our seniors stay in school, others are celebrations of homework completion, as we find that our students stop doing homework. The program adapts to help with whatever issues we find. If students are ditching, we celebrate attendance; if students are failing, we celebrate achievement; if they are not completing homework, we reward homework completion. We constantly tailor the program to meet our current needs.

BUG Program
Bring Up your Grades and Bug Out

The Renaissance Academic Incentive Program at one high school has a program that all students can participate in, whether they are 4.0 or .5 GPA students. It is called BUG, which stands for "Bring Up your Grades" and gives students incentives for increasing their GPA.

Here is how it works: The first 9-week grading period has just ended and grades have been distributed. The BUG program provides incentive for students who commit to raising their grades during the next grading period. After advertising and spreading the word about BUG over the past nine weeks, students have been coming in droves to the Counseling Center to pick up BUG contracts. The contract, printed on NCR paper, asks each student to identify up to three courses he/she wishes to target to "Bring Up" over the next nine weeks. The contract also requires that students identify several smart goals/steps that will help them achieve the higher grades. One stipulation on the contract is that no other course grade can drop a letter grade (grades can drop by a few points, but not by a whole letter grade). A neon green cover letter explains the program in detail. The students sign the contract, take it home to be reviewed and signed by a parent/guardian, and return it to the school counseling center. Even raising the percentage grade one point will mean a goal achieved.

Students who achieve their goals are recognized at an event they call BUG Out Day, where they receive incentives for each raised percentage grade. BUG Out Day is held the week after report cards are issued. Incentives include school imprinted items, Oops Coupons (forgotten homework and 5 test bonus points), free school store items, and of course, goodie treat bags.

14

"CAUGHT" Magnets
Catch and Celebrate Neat Lockers

Have you ever looked into a locker of a middle/high school student? It can range from a beautiful space that is organized and color coordinated to a bottomless pit of despair. A great way to transform your locker interiors from drab to fab is to have a CAUGHT program.

Every great administrator and guidance counselor walks the hallways in the morning as the students enter the building. This is an ideal opportunity to meet and greet the students and staff. As they walk the hallways, take note of some of the lockers that look great. Stop and talk with a student who has a great locker. Emphasize how the locker is organized and decorated. Don't worry about focusing on lockers that are not organized. Simply focus on the "WOW" lockers. As you talk with the student, be sure to write their name down and give them a "CAUGHT" magnet.

A "CAUGHT" magnet can be made very easily by your local merchandise printer. If you don't have a local printer, consider printing signs on business card paper and stick magnets on the back. Students love to have magnets in their lockers. Pick some fun exciting lettering and designs. The "CAUGHT" magnet is a great VTW recognition: it is Visible (other students can see it), Tangible (something they can keep and hold on to), and Walkaroundable (can be displayed in more than one location).

At the end of each day or week, take the names of the students who were "CAUGHT" and read them during your announcements, display them in the hallway, or show them on your internal television station. As the news spreads, you will be surprised how amazing and organized the lockers in your school will be. The end result of the "CAUGHT" program is that students are more organized, newsletters are going home and not ending up in the bottom of lockers, and students have a sense of pride about the school. Students can be "CAUGHT" doing the right thing.

College Signing Day and Wall
It's a Big Deal – Show It!

One of the biggest days for a college athlete is the day he/she signs with a professional team. On that day there are cameras, lights, fanfare, family and friends. When the announcement is made, everyone cheers as the contract is signed. Everyone has seen how ESPN makes it an amazing experience.

Within your school, set up an area where the students will have a college signing. Have the area decorated and set aside specifically for that purpose. If possible, have lights and the school video crew available. When the time is scheduled, announce the student's name and have them sign a "Letter of Intent" for the college they are attending. The same can be done for students attending a trade school or military. The local military recruiter would also love to support this activity. Following the signing, have photos of the student and the family placed in a dedicated location within the school.

Comeback Kid
From "On the Ropes" to "On the Stage"

Within our Renaissance program, we wanted to ensure that we recognized as many students as possible. We noticed that some students just don't make it academically. We also noticed that those students, as well as others, do improve. Therefore, we came up with the Comeback Kid recognition.

In order to be a Comeback Kid, a student moves up at least one grade level in any subject area. A student can move up from a B to an A or from an F to a D. Any move up makes the mark. Throughout the second marking period, we advertised the concept of Comeback Kid. The second marking period is best because they would have one set of grades as a starting point. Our advertisement for Comeback Kid was a photo of a student with a towel cape standing like a superhero. We talked about it during morning announcements every other day. We had posters all over the school. We sent notes and messages home through text and phone calls. The hype around the Comeback Kid was huge!

Every teacher wrote the name of each student who moved up one grade level in any subject. During the rally each Comeback Kid was announced and given a multi-colored wristband that had Comeback Kid on it. All the names of the Comeback Kids were posted in the hallways. We only posted the name and not the grade they moved up. With the wristband, teachers and students commented on the accomplishment.

The energy around improving and doing your best was contagious. Students were doing all they could to get the wristband and recognition. The next marking period we used a different color wristband. It was a silly advertisement and gimmick. Regardless of what it is, it worked! Grades went up and learning increased, all for a wristband and recognition as a Comeback Kid.

The Count
Make Multiplication Fun

One of the concerns the staffulty at my elementary school had was how the students were not able to learn the multiplication facts. Unlike when we were kids, there is not much time in the day or week to do multiplication drills with the students. Therefore, we decided to choose a number each week and read the multiplication facts from 0 to 12 during the morning announcements every day. So, I started reading these every day, and after the first week realized the kids were bored and I was getting tired. We decided to give it a Renaissance twist! Using my best "Count" from Sesame Street voice, I recorded all the multiplication facts onto a CD. A computer teacher then added thunder and special sound effects. We took a chance and played it during the morning announcements. It was a hit! All the students repeated the multiplication facts with a big smile on their faces.

Giant Wall Birthday Calendar
Recognize Every Student for at Least One Day

This idea is exactly what the title says it is. Locate a large empty wall within your school and measure out blocks similar to a monthly calendar. Then use blue painter's tape to tape off the blocks. At the start of the year cut out a bunch of stars or any shape that you want for each student. Have the students write their name on the front and birthday on the back.

Have a small committee of students organize the birthdays by month and then change it out each month by placing the names on the giant birthday wall. I was shocked how much the students loved it. Even some parents came by and took pictures of their child's name within the calendar. You could also use other shapes and highlight special events for the school on the calendar.

Good Citizen of the Month 2.0
Make the Criteria Public

This is a twist on something that a lot of schools do. Often schools have criteria for Citizen of the Month and they only share it with the staff so they can secretly look for students who fit that criteria. When the student is announced, it is a big surprise. Here is the switch: post the criteria for Citizen of the Month everywhere! Talk to the students about how important this honor is, and what is needed to become Citizen of the Month. The teachers should talk about it often and highlight those who are emulating the aspects of good citizenship. The end result is more students starting to show the behaviors of good citizenship in hope of winning the honor. True, there are those who will not care at all; but there are also those who will start moving in that direction, trying to get the award. Another option is to have former Citizens of the Month talk to the incoming freshman or students about the importance of the award and what they did/do to get and keep the honor.

GPA Championship
Bring Your Sports Teams' Competitiveness to Academics

The Team GPA Championship rewards the varsity team with the highest in-season GPA. All of the fall varsity sports compete against each other for the highest First Grading Period GPA. In the spring, varsity teams compete based on Third Grading Period GPA.

Here's how it works: coaches and captains are reminded of the competition at pre-season meetings. Reminders are also sent out at mid-grading period. Coaches are responsible for turning in rosters with GPAs listed by a certain deadline. The athletic director then checks to verify varsity status and GPAs.

Recognition for the highest team GPAs includes:

- Winners are announced via the sports board outside the gym, on morning TV announcements, at the academic or athletic pep rallies and any other appropriate venue
- Posters with names of winning teams are displayed next to the Team GPA banner in the gym for the entire year
- Players and coaches receive certificates
- Coaches receive a framed replica of the team poster
- Players receive Jostens Renaissance Platinum Cards
- Players receive T-shirts ("Team GPA Champs" is printed on the front, "Victory on the Field and in the Classroom" on the back). If a player is on two or three championship teams in one year, only one T-shirt is awarded and the duplicate winners get free movie passes, or something similar.
- A letter of congratulations is sent home and copied to the vice principal and guidance counselor for the student's file
- Championship teams are included in the "Athletic Achievement Brochure," which is published and mailed home at the end of the school year

This is a very competitive program that has made a strong connection between athletics and academics in our school. Not only has it been a positive program for our student athletes, but is has made our coaches become more actively involved in their athletes' academic lives.

Greeter
No More Hallway Duty

When you go to the Disney Store, who do you see standing at the entrance? That's right, a greeter. A greeter is used at the entrance to say hello to everyone and to make them feel good as they enter the store. I took the same concept and used it in the school for morning arrival. Teachers are assigned a location for morning hallway or bus duty. We simply change the name from hallway duty to morning greeter. The focus is to say hello to as many students as possible. You want to make the students feel happy and welcome to the school. We do not know what the students are coming to school with. Sharing a smile and a happy face may make all the difference in the world. This idea is 100% free! The greeter is still in charge of ensuring safety, but now with a smile and a high five.

H.A.T. Award
Random Recognition of Classes with Good Habits

H.A.T. stands for Homework/Attendance/Tardy. Randomly choose days and times to visit classrooms, preferably while wearing a silly hat. Politely ask to interrupt the classroom. Ask the teacher if everyone has their homework, there were no absences, and no one was tardy. If the answer is yes, explain to the class the importance of doing all the homework, being in school and not being late. Then leave a special treat for the class (such as doughnut holes, pencils, stickers, or temporary tattoos). If the answer is "no" to any of the questions asked, give the same speech about homework, attendance and being on time. Show the class what they would have gotten and move on to another classroom. After doing this randomly for a few weeks, the buzz will go around the school. Students don't know when it will happen and will start making the effort to not be "the one" to prevent the class from getting the treat.

Hard Work Cafe
Special Lunch Seating for Students Who Earn It

This idea has been around the world of Jostens Renaissance for a long time. There are many different versions of it. Basically, the concept is to provide a special eating location for students in the lunchroom and call it the Hard Work Cafe. How students get to sit in the Hard Work Cafe is up to you – it could be:

- Students with the best grades
- Citizen of the Week
- Nominated by teachers
- Students who asked the best questions
- Public Service Hours
- Homework

I have found that students don't want to eat in the Hard Work Cafe unless two things happen: (1) it is better than the table where they currently sit, and (2) they can bring a friend with them.

Bringing a friend is the easy part. Making it better than a normal lunch table experience is another thing. You could:

- Have real dishes and silverware for the students to use
- Have a special menu
- Have someone serve the meal to them
- Use table linens
- Separate it from the rest of the cafeteria
- Paint a mural on the wall
- Have a television showing fun shows
- Provide candy

21

- Offer special drinks or shakes

Hello Day
Take Student Orientation to the Next Level

Hello Day is a way to provide student orientation. Instead of students sitting in the auditorium listening to boring speeches about what they cannot do, the students are in the gymnasium on the floor moving and grooving and getting to know each other.

When the students come to school, they are ushered into the gymnasium to stay on the gymnasium floor. The parents are welcome to attend and they are ushered into the bleachers. There's an emcee for the students and a DJ to play fun, exciting music. The students on the floor are mixed up in as many different ways as possible. For example, move all the students wearing striped shirts to one side, solid colors to another side, and then they have to introduce themselves to as many other people as possible. Throughout the time we identify students for prizes and we take small groups out to the hallway to practice opening lockers for the first time. In between all of the fun and moving around, important messages are given to the students about the school that they need to know. After a little while watching the fun, the parents are moved into another location to be given information that they need to know about their child attending the school.

Near the end of the event, the parents are brought back into the gymnasium to watch the students continue to mix things up and play fun interactive games. The final activity is a rousing game of musical chairs with the parents. Musical chairs with parents is truly one of the funniest events you will ever see.

The best part about this event is that the students get an opportunity to truly enjoy and become one with the school. Teachers return for this in order to connect with their students. The students get an opportunity to practice opening lockers and see the school in a new light. Parents are reassured about sending their children to the school and word gets out that this school is different and truly focuses on students. Following all of the events, the students get the opportunity to go to their homeroom class. On the door of the classroom is a list of the students who will be in that classroom. It is amazing to see students' faces light up when they see that new friends they just met at Hello Day are now in their class.

Joke of the Day
The Unfunnier, the Better

Every morning during announcements I say the joke of the day. The joke is usually a goofy riddle that may or may not be funny. In fact, the ones that are not funny are the funniest. After saying the joke I laugh. Even if it is not funny, I laugh. This is done every day we have morning announcements. After doing this for the first few weeks, I knew I was on to something big. I started hearing students repeating the jokes in the hallways. Students would come to me with their own goofy jokes. Parents would share that each night at dinner they would ask what the joke of the day was. I even had substitute teachers excited to come to my school just to hear the joke of the day.

What's the big deal about the joke of the day?

The joke of the day sets the tone for learning throughout the day. It starts everyone on a positive note. Everyone likes a good joke. Everyone likes bad jokes too. Throughout the day, students and staff within the school could reflect back on the joke to give them a little pick-me-up whenever they needed it. The joke of the day is a great icebreaker for family discussion. Instead of parents starting the conversation with, "how was your day..." and the child responding, "it was okay..." The conversation starts with, "...tell me the joke of the day!" Instantly, dialogue starts and you have a worthwhile conversation.

Eventually, I purchased a mailbox and placed it outside of the main office where students, parents, staff, and community could leave jokes for me. If I said a student's joke during the announcements, they would get recognition and a small prize. Saying the joke of the day takes less than a minute. You do not have to be a good joke teller to do it. It will be even funnier if you don't know how to tell a joke. Below are a few of my favorite jokes. Additionally, my favorite joke book is *Jokelopedia*. This book has a ton of jokes that are categorized into topics.

How does a crazy person get through the forest?
He takes the psychopath!

What did the lightning bug say when he got stepped on?
I'm delighted!

Why are pirates so mean?
They just AAAARRRR!

What do you call cheese that doesn't belong to you?
Nacho Cheese!

Where does Captain Hook keep his treasure chest?
Under his treasure shirt!

Limo
Bring a Little Class to Your Main Entrance

There are many ways to use a limo to give recognition to students and staffulty.

- Park the limo in front of the school for the first day and have students climb in one side and out the other to look like they just arrived at the red carpet in a limo.
- Have a drawing from all students who were named "most improved" at the end of the marking period and give the drawing winner a ride to school in a limo.
- Park the limo in front of the school for a special event.

Even if it isn't used, it will make the event seem more important.

- Take the teacher of the year to lunch or dinner in the limo.
- Park the limo on the school grounds and fill with snacks for selected students to sit in it during lunch or break.
- Do the same thing for teachers during their prep time.

Locker Welcome Letter
Mission: Kindness

One year at my school we had the theme "Anything's Possible" based on the Mission Impossible movies. We had T-shirts and banners all over the school. Prepping for this theme was exciting – we had many fun events prepared for the school year. We needed to find a way to kick it off and surprise the students, so we printed small mission cards to place in each student locker. The mission cards had 25 different mission statements. Each card started with "Your mission, if you choose to accept it, is:" The statements were things like: Get to know a cafeteria worker. Meet two new people. Shake your teacher's hand every day for a week.

When the students arrived at school for the first day, they were surprised with a special "Mission" in their locker. The students were sharing with each other to see what mission they got. Some students taped it on the door of their locker as a reminder.

Lunch with the Principal
Make It More than Lunch

I have seen many schools offer lunch with the principal as a reward for students, especially at the elementary level. The first five minutes are fun, then it gets awkward and weird. The students start asking personal questions or revealing things that you just don't want to know. The principal runs out of things to compliment them on. Unless you have a fun activity planned, it turns into 30 minutes of torture. Here are some ideas to make lunch

25

with the principal bearable.

- Have trivia questions ready
- Play the *Are You Smarter Than a 5th Grader®* board game
- Share photos of your childhood (I did this and they LOVED it!)
- Play Bingo and make sure you are the caller
- Hire a magician (I did this and it was AWESOME!)
- Have Legos on the table and challenge them to build a transportation machine
- Watch *Schoolhouse Rock*
- Have coloring pages and colored pencils available
- Play "24" math game
- Play chess or checkers

Make It Matter Mondays
Take Time to Make Time

Every Monday, first thing in the morning! Have students take 2-5 minutes to reflect on how they will make this week matter. The students should be given time and encouragement to look at a calendar, organize their thoughts, and figure out a plan of action for the week. Consider asking them to write a statement about how they will make this week matter. Setting a goal and making a plan is a great way to start the week. Usually on Mondays, the focus is to Go, Go, Go! Often things get missed or one forgets something that may be important. Pulling out an extra five minutes to get it together at the start of the week can make all the difference. Consider these possibilities:

- Make a graphic organizer for the students to plan their week
- Have students do this in teams
- Provide two or three positive quotes they can use as a focus
- Leave a minute or two for some students to share

- Require that one goal or focus is to help someone else in some way
- Use check boxes to be able to check them off when things are done
- Do it on Google so that the teacher or guidance counselor can help keep him/her in check
- Use a positive word each week to focus the Make It Matter Monday

Money for a Cause
Choose Carefully and Do It Right

Throughout the school year, I am approached by many different organizations to help raise money for a worthy cause. As an educator, I understand the important life lessons about giving back that can be learned by the students. Unfortunately, we cannot approve every charitable group that comes knocking at our door. It would not be fair to overtax the students and community. Therefore, we decide at the start of the school year what organizations and charitable cause we will support. The success of our efforts determines if we will continue in the future.

Over the past four years my school has participated in the JDRF (Juvenile Diabetes Research Foundation) Kids Walk. Every year we have a group of students who live with type 1 diabetes. Because of this, we continue to support a JDRF Kids Walk. Part of my job to support the kids' walk is to motivate the students to raise money for the cause. This is done in three ways.

In-House Prizes: Whenever we support a cause, we never accept the student prizes that are offered to the students if they reach a certain level of fundraising. We feel that they will raise the money because it is the right thing to do, not because they will get a soccer ball or backpack. The prizes we offer are in house. We give the top homeroom a pizza party or gift certificate to the school store and snack line. Other options: principal for the day, homework pass, morning announcements, free entrance into a sporting event, or free entrance to a dance. The goal is to keep everything within the school.

Stand Out in the Crowd: Provide the opportunity for one or two students to stand out in the crowd. This offers students the opportunity to push their efforts to the next level. For the JDRF fundraising, I allow the top student in each grade level to throw a pie in my face in front of all of the other students on the last day of school. In order to build the excitement, I express how much I don't want to go through with this (knowing I am fine with it). Other options: silly string the principal, dunk tank, have the student lead the walk, photo opportunity in the newspaper, recognition at board meeting, photo posted on main bulletin board, morning announcements, medal or plaque. The focus is to provide the students a personal goal that allows them to shine.

Total Humiliation: The best way to get students excited about fundraising for a cause is to find a way to humiliate the leader of the school. First, set a goal that you want the students to reach. Then, find a way to make the leader look foolish. This year I told the students that if they reached the goal, I would come to school in a dress and blond wig. The students went nuts when I told them that. Other options: duct tape to the wall, camp on roof of the school, skydive, kiss a pig, dunk tank, wear short shorts and knee socks. Continue to advertise the humiliating act and chart the students' success.

The goal of fundraising for a cause is to teach the lesson of making a difference. Take the time before the school year starts to decide what charities you will participate in as a student body. By identifying early, it makes it easier to say no to other groups when necessary. If possible, keep the prizes in house. Identify ways to allow the top students to stand out and be recognized for their work. Someone needs to be humiliated! Preferably, the principal or school leader. Continue to advertise the humiliation and the reason for raising funds. Most important, have fun!

Morning Music
Set the Tone for the Day

If you are able to play music over the loudspeaker during morning arrival, it can make all the difference in the world. It truly sets the tone for the day. Look for a variety of music that is positive, upbeat or even slow in order to get the feeling you want. A great option would be to start the music in the morning at the same time with the same song. Once the music stops, the students must be in their homerooms ready to start the day. Over time, students will get used to the song as well as the amount of time. It is a great way to ensure that students will get to class on time.

Most Improved
They Work Hard all Year, So Recognize Them all Year

So often schools recognize the students who get the best grades or achieved sports greatness. How about the students who improve? Make sure you find ways to showcase the students who have made gains such as these:

- Moved up one grade level
- Moved up .5 on a 4.0 grading scale
- Decreased disciplinary actions
- Read more books
- Moved up two grade levels
- Turned in 100% homework for the first or second time
- Increased class participation

Don't wait until the end of the school year to recognize the students who have made improvement. Consider at the end of each grading cycle or the end of each month. Either way it is all about encouraging those who would otherwise not be recognized.

Name-Calling Week
Make it Positive!

One elementary school's Renaissance program turned name-calling into a positive thing! Every student and staff member chose a "name" that reflected a positive personal trait. Then, all students and staff made name tags and wore them all week so others could address them positively. Examples included:

Understanding
Hopeful
Funny
Nice
Athletic
Intellectual
Talented
Compassionate
Happy
Beautiful

Throughout the week, and beyond, students and staff had fun AND received a self-esteem boost. Students and staff empowered each other and felt empowered themselves by turning name-calling into something positive.

Parade of Success
Start the Year with a Celebratory Walk

Either on the first day of school or the next day, have a parade around the neighborhood to celebrate the start of school. When I was a principal of a lower elementary school, that is exactly what we did.

The weeks before school started, we drafted a letter to give to the residents who live along the route we were going to walk. The letter informed them that we would be walking to celebrate the start of school, and invited them to come out and wave to the children as they walk by. We contacted the local fire department and they provided a fire truck to lead the parade. In the welcome back letter to the students, we informed them that we will have a parade around the block to celebrate the start of school. If any parent did not want their child to participate, they were asked to let us know. Each classroom decorated a class flag, so that when it was time to have the parade, each classroom had a flag to represent them. At the end of the event everyone gathered in front of the school. A few encouraging words were said and everyone returned to class.

The event was enjoyed by everyone. The community came out to wave to the children and all the students had smiles. We even got in the newspaper! The entire event took about 1 hour.

Passing the Torch Ceremony
Make Leadership Visible

On the last day of school, I would hold a pep rally to recognize the accomplishments of the students and staff over the last marking period and to celebrate the school year. Halfway through the rally we would pause for the Passing the Torch Ceremony. On one end of the gymnasium would be the outgoing student government leadership with the school mascot. On the other side of the gymnasium was the incoming student government leadership. The outgoing student leaders would each have a tiki torch with paper flames on the top. I would inform the students that it is now time for the Passing the Torch Ceremony. I would talk about the great things that took place over the school year and how much they have earned the right to move up to the next grade level.

I ask all students and staff to stand up for the Passing the Torch Ceremony. I explain that once the torch is passed from the current student leadership to the new student leadership, they will officially be in the next grade level. I give them one minute to celebrate. The music starts to play the theme from "Chariots of Fire." The student leadership slowly starts to walk around the

31

perimeter of the gymnasium. Once they make it back to the far end of the gym, they start to walk slowly toward each other. Once in the middle of the gym, they wave the torches in the air and pass it to the new leaders. Instantly, the music switches to the song "Walking on Sunshine." I yell "Congratulations!" and the students cheer, yell and dance. What they don't know is that each teacher has a can of silly string that they have been hiding. The teachers instantly turn to the students and start to spray with silly string. For one minute it is complete celebrating craziness. The students are ecstatic that they have moved up and the teachers have one final fun time with their current students.

Pinning Ceremony
Start Freshman Year with Formality

On the night that the incoming freshmen go for the orientation at one technology high school, they review what to expect. There are musical selections and upper classmen giving speeches about how they felt the first day of school and how they made it through. Following all the information and welcome speeches, they have all the new incoming freshmen line up against the wall. Standing on the stage are the students who spoke, administrators, and a few teachers. Ten students at a time go up on stage, meet with the school representatives and receive a pin with the school name on it. This pin represents their official admittance to the school. As the students are getting their pin, the parents are encouraged to take photos and there is fun music playing in the background. Following the pinning ceremony, there is a reception with refreshments and the different clubs showcasing their membership. The new freshmen are proudly wearing their new pins.

Positive Office Referral
Give Them a Good Experience in the Office

When a student misbehaves, he/she is written up on an office referral form, which has been designed to provide clarification to the office of what the infraction was. There are categories that determine how serious of an action it was and guidance on how to handle it. Usually only students getting in trouble are called to the office. With a Positive Office Referral, staffulty can write up any student for doing the right thing. The Positive Office Referral form categorizes good behavior so the office can understand what was done. I asked the teachers to send at least one Positive Office Referral a month, but most did two or three. The office administrator would always call down the student and ask him/her if he/she knew why he/she was there? Most of the time they had no idea and were on the verge of crying. The administrator would read the positive referral and praise the student for his or her actions. It is important to call the student's parent while the student is in the office, then share the news with the parent and pass the phone to the student so they can talk. On many occasions, everyone in the room and on the phone was in tears. During the recognition rally, all the students who received Positive Office Referrals were recognized again.

Rally Theme Ideas
Use These, or Come up with Your Own!

Beach
Pirate
Cool 2 Care
Hero Within
Egypt
Hounds on the Loose
Hawaii
Olympics
You're a STAR
Out of This World
Star Wars
Wild West
Superstar Treatment
Sports

Ring the Bell
Kick Things Off in Classic Style

Think back to the 30s, 40s, and 50s. Think back when there were no computers, electronic bell schedules, and ID cards. Back then the students knew school would start by hearing the ringing of a hand-held bell. That bell was used to start school, start recess, end recess and end school. The bell had a distinct sound. When you heard it, you knew what to do.

Go out and get a bell just like the ones used "back in the day." Use the bell to officially start events at your school. Specifically, use the bell on the first day of school. Before opening the doors to allow all the students into the building, gather the staff in the front of the school, say a few prepared words, then ring the bell. True, some of the kids may look at you a little funny, but the parents and staff will smile with affection.

Continue to use the bell to start events at your school. Use the bell for an assembly, kick off field day, or start the spelling bee. Additionally, use the bell to signify the end of each marking period, the end of state testing, the end of field day, and the end of the school year. After some time everyone will expect to hear the bell before and after special events. It will turn into a tradition at your school.

Roll Out the Red Carpet
Treat Them Like Royalty

Every school should have a Red Carpet! Go to the local carpet store and explain that you need a long red carpet runner that is durable. As a school, you may get it at a reduced rate or free. You can use the red carpet for all kinds of important events at the school. The students love it and it makes the event seem even bigger than it truly is. Have paparazzi on either side of the carpet taking photos of students and include them in the yearbook. Use it for:

- First day of school
- Back to School Night with parents
- New student introduction
- Academic rally
- Teacher professional development
- Visitors to your school
- Prom
- Homecoming
- Awards assembly
- National Honor Society induction
- Random day at School
- Kindergarten registration
- Kick off a fundraiser event

Secret Star
Surprise Them with Prizes

Cut out a star and place it under the chair of one student in each classroom either before school or the night before. If the chairs are up, put it under the desk. During morning announcements, state the importance of getting to school on time and what it means to be a star. Then state that there is one secret star under a chair/desk in each classroom, and that person is the winner and should come to the office for a prize. The prize can be anything from a button to a t-shirt – anything that can be seen by others. Do this randomly throughout the school year. As soon as the students forget about it, do it again! Another option would be to do this for back to school night – parents love it! Make sure the prize is a good one. Teachers also love this for staffuly meetings and professional development training.

Show My Name
Simple Recognition for the Cost of Poster Board

I wish I started this the first year I started teaching. The concept is so simple yet makes a huge impact. At the end of the marking period or semester, identify the students who received high marks and place their names on a list. Take that list and have it printed into a poster – if your school has a poster maker, use it. Hang the posters in a prominent location in the school. The pride that the students have in seeing their name is extremely high. Parents come in to see their child's name. You can post students' names for any positive reason. The most important part is to rotate the names as each marking period or semester goes by.

Student Perfect Attendance Lunch
Showing up can Earn a Steak Meal

One Renaissance group recently celebrated True Perfect Attendance with 21 students who were present every day, every class last semester. The students were encouraged to invite one friend to enjoy a steak dinner and preferred seating with the principal. Steaks were prepared by an assistant principal, and the computer lab clerk organized the luncheon for the students and their guest. The students and their guest enjoyed a steak, potato, salad, tea and their choice of ice cream as their reward for having True Perfect Attendance.

That's My Spot
Let Seniors Personalize Their Parking Spaces

A great recognition for seniors who are allowed to drive to school is to allow them to paint their parking spot. Each senior who is allowed to drive is assigned a specific spot in the student parking lot. In the summer, before the start of school, choose a day for the seniors to come and paint their spot with any design they want (within reason). They must provide their own paint. Explain what kind of paint would work best. At the end of the school year, paint over each spot with black paint to provide a clean slate for the next senior. It will become a powerful rite of passage for the entire student body and there will be no conflict over whose spot is whose.

Thinking Caps
The Power of Suggestion

When you really need to think in elementary school, what does the teacher tell you to do? That's right, put on your thinking cap. Usually, the kids pull out the imaginary cap and pull it down on their heads. Why not make one? At one elementary school, I went out and got a bunch of painters' caps with the school name printed on them. The students then were able to decorate the caps however they wanted. The caps stayed in the school. Whenever the students needed to think hard, they would pull out their thinking caps and have at it. We ended up using the caps for state testing. The students were sure that they were smarter with the caps on. If that is what it took to make the students concentrate and do their best, then I would make sure they wore their thinking caps.

Valet Service
Arriving Should Feel Special

This idea will add a touch of class to the first day. As the students are dropped off by the parents in the morning, have some selected staff open the car doors and welcome the students to the first day of school. For high schools that have students who drive, have staff greet students in the student parking lot and open the doors for them once they park. This will put a huge smile on the students' and parents' faces. It reassures the parents that everything will be fine and allows the school to send a positive message. Some options could be:

- Wear a brim hat and white gloves
- Give each parent a small paper quote to motivate them for the day
- Acknowledge each student as "Madam" or "Sir"
- Offer to clean the car windows (if time allows)
- Have a balloon tied to wrist to bring attention to the staff member

Week of Recognition
Making Connections Every Day

Here are ideas that you can implement into your classroom each day for one week. The focus of the ideas is to improve the environment in the classroom and maintain positive relationships with your students. They are easy and quick! Try them out and share with me how the students responded to them and the tone in the classroom. Enjoy!

Monday: High Five! Give each student a high five as they enter the room. Everyone knows what a high five is. It takes the general basic hello and makes it more exciting. Also, doing this as the students enter the room sets the tone for your time together. The atmosphere is upbeat and positive. This may be a shock to your students if you don't usually greet your students as they enter. Try it out!

Make sure you have a bottle of hand sanitizer close by after touching hands with so many kids. Another option is to give a fist bump.

Tuesday: Share a Story: Think of a positive story you were involved in when you were a child and share it with the class. It doesn't have to be a super motivational story. It just has to be about you. Your students are very interested in who you are and who you were. Making connections with your students is important. This is an opportunity to let them see the non-teacher side of you. Be careful not to get sucked into a full class discussion about childhood events. You don't need a smooth segue to blend into the lesson. Just share the story and move on into the lesson.

Wednesday: Ask a Question: At the start of class, tell the students you will give an award to the student who asks the best question for the lesson. The award doesn't have to be elaborate. It can be as simple as a paper ribbon. The focus is to recognize the educational efforts of the students in the class and stretch their thinking. As each student asks a question, make sure you acknowledge the question and prompt others to "up the ante." Also make sure you have a great lesson for the students to ask questions. Don't do this if you are planning on reviewing simple math facts. Try the intro to a new subject or review before a test.

Thursday: Shake a Hand: As the students leave the class, shake each one's hand. Thank them for their efforts during the class. Make sure you do it right. Give a firm handshake, look in the eyes, and speak clearly. True, some students will think it is weird. Some students would appreciate the gesture. It gives a positive closure to the lesson and your time together. Make sure you have a bottle of hand sanitizer close by after touching hands with so many kids.

Friday: Quote: Write a motivational quote on the board before the students enter the room. Make sure the quote is written big enough on the board for everyone to see. Take a minute or two and discuss the meaning of the quote. Don't turn it into a lesson. Just talk about the quote and give the students time to talk about it. Be careful not to get sucked into a full class discussion about the quote that prevents your lesson from being taught. The point is to set the tone for the lesson and establish the direction for the day.

Welcome Wagon
Recognize Arrivals and Departures

How are new students welcomed to your school? In most cases, new students get to see the person who registers them in the guidance office, then are given a schedule, walked down to a room, and left to fend for themselves. As the year progresses, those new students may or may not connect with the school community.

When a student leaves a school, what is the process for the student to feel recognized and remembered? The student leaving may have been with the district and fellow peers for many years and have deep connections with other students. When the student leaves, he/she just wants someone to recognize the time they spent at the school and be sent off with smiles.

New Students: When a new student registers at the school during the school year it is an opportunity for the school to truly welcome the new student into the fold. Prepare a large envelope with an image of a wagon on the front and the words "Welcome Wagon." Inside the envelope are the following types of items:

- Parent Handbook/Student Handbook
- List of important names of people in the school
- Student Government officer names and pictures
- Bell schedule/Map of school
- Agenda planner (with handwritten welcome from principal would be a nice touch)
- Community pizza shop menu
- Principal and vice principal business cards
- School car magnet
- School store coupon
- Lunch room snack coupon

It is a MUST that the principal meets the student face to face and welcome him/her to the school. Making that connection is vital for the new student to connect with the school. Don't let the new student's first connection be with anyone else except the number one supporter of the school, the principal. Additionally, the vice principal, guidance counselor, head custodian, etc. can also welcome the student.

Departing Students: When a student leaves the school, he/she wants others to notice that he/she left. Here are a few ways to let the student know that he/she will be remembered:

- Take his/her picture and post on a bulletin board. Title the board the "See You Soon" or "Still a Cougar" board.
- Have a page in the yearbook to highlight those who left during the year
- Send a farewell text to the student

- Make sure the student is signed up to get school notifications via email or text so he/she knows what is going on
- Get new address and send an invitation to student for homecoming

Yard Sign
Recognize Students Publicly

We've all seen bumper stickers that say "My Child is an Honor Student." What if you provided yard signs that conveyed the same message to neighbors and students? Have the signs made and sell them to parents who have a child who made honors. The sign can be for all kinds of recognition of the students. You can also make a yard sign for graduation or college acceptance.

You Made a Difference
Seniors Offering Thanks

This is a great idea for graduating seniors. Have the students identify a person who made a difference in their life, then write a letter explaining why that person made such an impact. Have certificates made that the students can give to the special person. Set a day near the end of the school year to allow the seniors to visit the special person and hand deliver the letter and certificate. It will be a heartfelt day and strengthen connections. When the students return to school, have them get together in small groups and share the experience. This is an awesome way to wrap up the high school experience, both for students and for those who helped them.

Take It From Me: Courage

What exactly is courage? What are the elements of courage? Who shows courage? The best way to define courage is to understand what makes courage happen. The one and only thing that makes courage happen is one of the strongest and powerful emotions. The answer is not love or compassion, but fear. Yes, fear! Right now many of your eyebrows are moving up and down on your face thinking about what was just stated. It's true, when someone is faced with a challenge that he/she is unsure about or an obstacle that seems impossible, the first emotion that comes forward is uncertainty, doubt, or confusion. That all adds up to fear! Then something amazing happens. The negative emotions get pushed aside and courage comes forward to save the day. The ultimate question is: how can we move fear aside and be more courageous more often? Below are three ways to be more courageous.

Strength in Numbers: Doing it alone is always harder than working as a group or team. You do not have to go through life's challenges locked arm and arm with your support group (although it makes for a great visual); the support group may be just what it says: support. Surround yourself with those who celebrate you, not tolerate you. I'll say it again – surround yourself with those who celebrate you, not tolerate you. It is easier to be courageous if you know that in the end, others who are close to you will appreciate you. Additionally, if you fail, those who are close to you may benefit and appreciate your efforts.

It's All About WE: In most cases, times of courage affect not only you but others as well. Very often courage comes about through interactions with others and others are counting on you. Knowing that others are viewing your actions can allow you to step up your game and take your actions to a new level. Very rarely is courage an "I" occurrence. Usually courage is a "WE" event. Pull strength from the desire to help others in order to face the fear and be courageous.

Back to the Future: Think about the experiences you have had in your life. Think about the failures you have had. Think about the successes you have had. All of those things within your past are fuel for courage. The failures you had in your life are strong life lessons that allow you to think about how to be strategic and think logically. Your failures should prevent you from doing something foolish instead of courageous. Your successes empower you to take chances and take the leap of faith. All of those things make you who you are and help you be courageous.

Keep in mind that the fear usually doesn't go away through the process of being courageous. Hopefully, in the end, you come out victorious. Courage is stronger than fear. It is stronger than anything because even though you might falter and stumble, courage is what picks you up again, dusts you off, and sets you on your way to make a difference and to be the best person that you can possibly be.

"Courage is the first of human qualities because it is the quality which guarantees all others." – Winston Churchill

"Courage is being afraid but going on anyhow." – Dan Rather

Staffulty Fulfillment

Appy Hour
An App Shared is an App Squared

Invite teachers throughout the district to come together for a specific date and time to share the very best teacher apps they use to help them with instruction in the classroom. Boom! Mind blown!

B44
Bond with New Teachers

As principal I felt it was my duty to connect, train, and guide my newer non-tenured teachers. It would be irresponsible of me not to share my vision and goals with them and purposefully position them for success. With that in mind, I created the B44 group within my school.

B44 stands for Before Four Years. All teachers who have taught in Hartford School for less than four years are welcome to join. We meet once a month in one of the teacher's classrooms. This group is completely voluntary. B44 is separate from the new teacher training series within the district. The goal of B44 is to allow time for the non-tenure teachers to have access to me and building administration. During this time, I will share with them my vision of education and the school. It is a very open environment. The discussion flows both ways. During our time together we discuss articles, look at videos, answer questions, explain decisions made, introduce key people in the district, and anything else that may come up. We don't necessarily talk about lesson plans, curriculum, and specific assessment strategies. It mostly revolves around the vision, goals, and what makes the school, the school.

Think of it this way: hopefully, the new teachers will stay in your school for many years. Why not take the time at the start of their career to develop a strong personal bond? Don't leave it up to chance. As the years go by, you continually strengthen the relationships with your new staff. Ten to fifteen years down the line, you will have a very strong staff that understand the vision and have powerful, positive relationships with administration.

Believe It or Not
Getting to Know Each Other Better

This is a great way to connect the staff with each other. Prior to a staffulty meeting send out an email to everyone to have them think about something that nobody knows about them but that they are willing to share with others. Have a poster taped to the wall in the faculty room with "Believe It or Not" written on the top. Throughout the day, instruct staff to write statements about themselves that others wouldn't believe, but not to include their names. When the staffulty meeting comes, start the meeting with everyone guessing who wrote which statement. Eventually, have the people reveal themselves. You are guaranteed laughs and smiles. Take the posters and re-post them in the staffulty lounge. They will talk about it for weeks.

Birthday Ambush
Start Your Birthday Right

Our students came up with this idea in order to celebrate the teachers' birthdays. I gave the student leader of the group a list with the name of each teacher and his or her birthday (not including the year). A small group of students get together in the morning and ambush the teacher in his or her classroom with a happy birthday song. Following the song, they slap a poster on the door that says, "I've been birthday ambushed! Happy Birthday!"

After the first three teachers got ambushed, it caught on like wildfire. Teachers were excited and could not wait for their turn. Even the teachers who have birthdays during the summer were checking in to see when they would get their ambush. It was a simple little thing, but it went a long way because the kids recognized their birthdays and left a poster so they would get good wishes all day.

BYOB
Liven up your Faculty Meetings

BYOB stands for Bring Your Own Banana. This is a fun twist to a faculty meeting. Prior to the meeting, put a banana in each faculty member's mailbox. You can even write on the banana instructions that they must bring the banana with them to the faculty meeting. Once the teachers arrive at the meeting, have ice cream and toppings available for them. Starting off the faculty meeting with everyone having a banana split is a great way to end the school day and start the meeting.

Caf Staff
The School Runs on its Stomach

How often do you recognize your cafeteria staff? Yes, they are a part of the school family as well. It doesn't matter if your food services are contracted out or not. They matter. Each month take a photo of a cafeteria worker and post it on a board. Ask some questions about him/her to get interesting information to post with the photo. Make sure you highlight the posting during your announcements so that the school family will take notice. It is a small gesture that will go a long way.

Other options:

- Highlight the cafeteria workers in your parent newsletter or school newspaper
- Have a bulletin board with the names and faces of all workers

- Give them a staff T-shirt
- Remember to let them know when special events take place
- Always invite them to faculty meetings (even if you know they won't go)
- Include them in staff appreciation activities
- Thank you letters from students
- Thank you letters from staff
- Place thank you notes in the kitchen the night before so they see it when they come in the next day
- Secretly tell the students that it is National Smile at a Cafeteria Worker day. Do it all day and see whether they notice.

Custodial Staff Recognition
"Sing" for the Unsung Heroes

Every night when everyone leaves the school and the hallways and classrooms are empty, something amazing happens. A very dedicated and focused group of unsung heroes appear in the school and start the tedious job of cleaning the building. That's right, I'm talking about your custodial staff.

One of the most important groups within your school is the custodial and maintenance staff. It doesn't matter if they are members of the district or contracted to an outside company. They are very important to the cleanliness and safety of the school. The school would not run if it were not for them. I am sure there are plenty of horror stories regarding how some of the rooms and hallways appear. Nevertheless, just imagine how it would look if nothing was ever done?

What I have done in my building to recognize the custodial staff is to simply post a sign in the hallway that states, "The cleanliness of this wing is maintained by: _____." This one simple gesture changes everything. Once you post this sign in the hallway, you are allowing the custodians to show pride in their work.

Now everyone knows who keeps this hallway clean. For the hallways that are not so clean, this puts a name to the not-so-clean hallway. I assure you, things will start looking better once a name goes up. If you want to take it to the next level, get a photo of the custodial staff and place it with the sign. Now a name and a face are attached to the hallway.

When I posted the signs, each of the custodial staff came to me to say thank you and good idea. The director of grounds, business director, assistant superintendent, and superintendent all appreciated the signs. Take the time – say thank you to your custodial and maintenance staff.

Dress Down Mondays
Start the Week with a Break

The title of this idea says it all. Typically, schools and companies offer dress down Fridays. There is nothing wrong with that. It is a great way to celebrate a hard week of work and prepare for a fun weekend. On dress down Fridays people are feeling good, as if nothing can bother them for the day. The weekend is looking good and all is well.

Just think of what would happen if on Friday afternoon an email or an announcement was made by the principal that Monday is a dress down day. Instantly, people would start popping out of their rooms like gophers from the ground, buzzing with each other about the dress down day for Monday. All of a sudden people are dancing in the hallways, skipping to their cars, and going out for drinks. The weekend is full of vigor and anticipation for the upcoming workweek. The best thing is that everyone is ready for Monday to come.

Usually, Monday is a day that drags and people are not full of much energy. But on Dress Down Monday people are upbeat and comfortable. What a great way to start off the week! Keep in mind that you don't want to pull this card out that often. Just when you see that things are tense or stress levels are getting high is a good time to use a Dress Down Monday. Talk to your school or company leadership and try it out. It doesn't cost a thing!

Heart to Heart Award
Encourage Staffulty to Recognize Each Other

This award is for the staffulty only and involves an old bowling pin. It starts with giving the bowling pin to a teacher and explaining that at the next staffulty meeting he/she is to give the bowling pin to another teacher. At the start of the staffulty meeting, explain that a new award is starting. That teacher gets up and says something nice about the person he/she is giving it to and then hands the person the bowling pin award. That person is to hold the bowling pin for one month and then give the pin to another person who has made an impact in some way.

What was interesting was that as each person passed the pin on they added something to the pin. They added stickers, glasses, hair, and face. By the end of the school year it didn't look like a bowling pin at all – it took on new meaning. This award became the most cherished award among the staffulty, because it came from the heart.

Honorary Diplomas
Seniors Recognizing Those Who Made it Possible

One high school has an annual tradition of allowing the graduating seniors to give an honorary diploma to any teacher or staff they wish. The diploma can be given to any staff member from elementary, middle, or high school. The recipient does not have to be a classroom teacher – he or she could be an aide, custodial staff, or secretary. The focus of the diploma is to recognize how that person has contributed to the success of the senior.

In the spring, once the students get their cap and gown, the school dedicates a day for the seniors to go around the district and deliver the diplomas. The seniors arrive dressed in their cap and gown to deliver the diploma. When delivering the diploma, the senior shares his/her story about why the person contributed to the success.

Last Day Ice Cream
Celebrate Summer with a Treat

On the last day of school, after the students pull away on the buses, give your staffulty a treat. Schedule to have the local ice cream truck come by the school that day, and encourage each staffulty member to get one ice cream treat from the truck. This is a great way to say thank you for a great school year.

Life Saver
Say Thanks with Sweets

Go to your local bulk grocery store and get a large box of Life Saver candies. Make labels with a supportive message to the staff, along the lines of "Thanks for all you do. You are a true Life Saver." Put the candy in the teacher mailboxes in the evening, and get ready for smiles the next morning. Some other options:

- Payday bar on the first payday of the school year
- 100 Grand bar for those who are named teacher of the month
- Kudos bar for those who go above and beyond
- Mints with a note saying, "You are worth a mint!"
- Milky Way or Orbit gum with a note saying, "You are out of this world!"

Out of the Office Day
See and Be Seen, All Around the School

One of the challenges for administrators is getting away from paperwork and being stuck in the office. Yes, it is important to get the office work done and there are deadlines that must be met. When administrators get out of the office, it is usually for an observation, walk through, or solving an issue. Out of the Office Day is a dedicated day to stay out of the office and to visit classrooms, students, and staffulty for no reason but to visit. There is never a perfect day to do this, so just pick a day and go for it. It is important to notify your staff ahead of time that this is your official Out of Office Day. Make sure they know you are around just to enjoy the school. No formal observation. No follow up conversation. No responding to emails. Have the office secretary be aware and "hold down the fort." If you are fortunate and have other administrators on staff, have them cover for you for the day. Once you get over the anxiety of being away from the office, you will find it to be one of the most rewarding days of the year.

Para Recognition
See Your "Invisible" Staff

Each month I have a faculty meeting with my teaching staff. I also have a monthly meeting with my aides/paraprofessionals. Honestly, how many of you have meetings scheduled for your aides/paraprofessionals monthly? The focus of the meetings revolves around three parts.

- One: Share important information about the school. Yes, they are invited to attend the regular faculty meeting. Yes, I could put it in a memo. No, that's not good enough. This provides time for the school leadership to connect with them and to make them feel special.
- Two: Provide training to the aides/paraprofessionals and share the vision of the school. This is the perfect oppor-

tunity to directly share with them what you expect from everyone in the school. Provide scenarios that may challenge their thinking and discuss how they would handle it. Then express what your expectations are.

- Three: Give them a voice. If you talk to any aide/para-professional, they will say the number one complaint is that they are invisible and not respected. Remember, aides/paraprofessionals see EVERYTHING! They are in many classrooms, lunchrooms, and hallways. They know what is good and what is not. Give them the time to voice their feelings and observations. You may be able to resolve many issues by simply sitting back and listening.

Pat on the Back
To Make Sure You Get One, Do It Yourself!

Have you ever had a moment in time when you said something or did something amazing, but nobody was around to see it? How about when you worked through a difficult problem with little to no help from anyone else? Better yet, have you ever accomplished a goal that you have set for yourself that nobody else knew you were shooting for?

If you said yes to any one of the above questions, you are not alone. Yet actually, you are alone! That is the problem. We all know how important it is to provide recognition to others when they do well. Who is there to recognize you when you have done something great? Often you are alone. You would like to share with others your triumph, but you feel like you would be bragging or boasting about your accomplishment.

You need to make sure you take the time to give yourself a pat on the back. I printed the copy of my hand and placed it on the wall. Whenever I do a good job with something, I walk over to my hand on the wall, turn around facing away, and give myself a pat on the back. It only takes a few seconds to push my back against my hand and say "good job" to myself.

It is vitally important that you praise yourself when you do a good job. You are your best advocate. You can also be your worst critic. So often people put themselves down and look at everything they cannot do. I am giving you permission to celebrate you! It is not vain. It is not cocky. It is not arrogant. It is personal time to motivate yourself and keep the fire alive.

Another option with this idea is to cut out small hands. Share the story of giving someone a pat on the back. Students can purchase a "Pat on the Back" hand as part of a school fundraiser. Write the name of the person who receives it on the back and have them delivered.

Substitutes
How to be Their First Choice School

How do you support your substitutes? Yes, I said substitute teachers. Day in and day out, they come to "fill in" for your absent teachers. The way I see it, as school principal, I want the very best substitutes. Additionally, I never want to be without substitutes. I remember days when I would be short several substitutes and I had to be creative in order to cover all classes. That does not happen anymore. Now, I have every available substitute running into my school and doing all they can to stay. Here is what I do:

Hello: In the morning as teachers and substitutes arrive to school, I try to stand by the front counter where the sign in sheet is. I make it a point to say hello to every substitute who enters the main office. As you know, there are some substitutes who are regulars. They are at the school so often they are like one of the staff. I make sure I greet them with the same excitement as all the other substitutes. A simple hello can mean so much. If there is a new substitute that I have not seen before, I make it a point to shake his/her hand and welcome him/her. If I am able I will do quick introductions of others in the office that could provide assistance. Often the school secretary does the introductions, but I do whenever I can.

How's it going? Throughout the day, whenever I see a substitute, I ask, "How's it going?" I'll be honest: sometimes I don't want to know. It would be so much easier to walk by with a smile and a nod. At times I force myself to ask how they are doing. Most of the time they say, "fine." Every now and then they give me some details about a difficult class. Immediately, I am on the walkie-talkie to get support or walk into the classroom to show my presence. The focus is to provide support and make sure they feel appreciated.

Hang your hat: There are times when substitutes have to travel from room to room. Because of the traveling schedule, they have to carry all of their things with them throughout the day. The other option is to ask one of the classroom teachers to place their things in the classroom and hope the teacher is in the room so they can get their things at the end of the day. What I have done is get a set of portable lockers and place them against the wall in the upstairs teachers' lounge. Additionally, I had a coat rack placed in the same room. Substitutes are informed that they are welcome to keep their things in the lockers in the teachers' room and hang their coat/hat on the coat rack. Some of the regular substitutes bring a small lock and key with them in order to secure their materials. This is a very easy accommodation that is greatly appreciated by the substitutes.

Here is a shirt: If I have a substitute who is a regular and we can always depend on, I give him/her a staff shirt. This is huge to a substitute. Once I give a substitute a staff shirt, he/she is committed to our school. I know that every time we have an opening, I am guaranteed to have at least one person that will be here in body, mind, and soul. As a principal, that is what I want.
Through this simple process I have the most dedicated and competent substitutes available. I have had many substitutes say to me that they will pick my school over any other school on the

roster. They make that commitment because they don't feel invisible and do feel appreciated.

Support the Support
The Community Talks to Them First

Support staff is vitally important to the success of the school. Custodians, food service workers, classroom aides, and bus drivers have extremely important jobs. If any one of them were unable to do their job, the entire place would fall apart. Additionally, they can provide great information to the community about your school. Therefore, they should always be kept in the loop. They should know what is going on and what their role is in the bigger picture.

Give them the stuff: Make sure they get the parent newsletter, staff newsletter, all email messages, staff handbook, phone messages, and text alerts. They should receive it the same day as everyone else. They should never be considered an afterthought.

Meetings: If you are able to, invite them to the regular faculty meeting. If you are unable to, schedule a special meeting for them. I schedule a standing support staff meeting every month. It is voluntary and some months I have a full house, other months I have two people. Either way, I am there with an agenda and quality information.

Come see me: The principal should schedule a time every month when support staff can visit with the principal. It is a clearly advertised time that is just for support staff to communicate with the principal about whatever they wish.

Training: If possible, provide professional development on public relations for support staff. Often support staff is the first encounter with the community. Make sure it is a good one.

Within Disney World®, the street cleaners are trained on customer service more than any other position. The reason is because they are mixed within the public more than any other position. Therefore, they are approached by more people and are asked more questions than anyone else. Disney realized that they want to make every experience within the parks magical, even talking with support staff.

Teacher Appreciation Week Ideas
Show Teachers You Care, and Show Students how it's Done

Mug Monday (Teachers get a coffee mug and free coffee)
Taco Tuesday (Make your own taco at lunch)
Wet Wednesday (Non-alcoholic mixed drinks at lunch)
Thank You Thursday (Students wrote thank you notes to teachers)
Final Friday Dress Down (Everyone likes comfortable clothes)

Tenure Done Right
It's a Big Deal – Make it One!

If you are a tenured teacher or administrator, think back to the day you got tenure. I am sure it was filled with excitement, joy, and celebration. The many gifts and congratulations were overflowing. You could barely contain the excitement. NOT!

For most of us, the day we got tenure was like any other day of work. Yes, a few people may have congratulated you. Possibly you got a plant from the union. A select few got a handshake from an administrator.

I challenge you to think of tenure as a milestone and powerful rite of passage. Getting tenure states that as a school, as a district, and as a community, we trust you. We feel that you are able to instruct the children to the level we expect. It states that you've got the "Right Stuff"! Therefore, when someone gets tenure, it should be celebrated and recognized appropriately. Here are four ways to recognize your staff when they obtain tenure.

Tea anyone? Have a Tenure Tea. Invite the staff that has obtained tenure to a special Tea or lunch. Taking the time to break bread together and express how important they are to the school community goes a long way. The Tea or lunch can be in the school or out at a local restaurant. Try connecting with the restaurant to get a discounted meal and have a special sign at the reserved table congratulating those being honored.

In the news: Contact the local paper and have an ad showcasing the tenured teachers. Have a big "Congratulations!" as the headline with the names underneath. Don't forget to show the names on the school marquee, bulletin boards, school newsletter, school website, school Facebook page, and Twitter. The focus is to show everyone how much it means to get tenure in your district.

Just for you: Go to your local embroidery store and get an item embroidered with the tenured teacher's name on it. Having a special item that signifies this event will mean a great deal to each educator who gets one. There are many items that can be personalized, including: pens, trophies, glass apples, desk signs, plaques, letter jackets, Superman capes, school bells, mascot ornaments, and class rings.

Come see me: If you are an administrator, take the time to meet with each tenured staff on the day they get tenure. Make sure the meeting is private with no interruptions. Explain why you hired him/her. Share some funny stories that you both can reminisce about. Outline your future expectations and say how proud you are to be working with him/her. This meeting will be burned into the educator's memory. It is an important opportunity to solidify the administrator-educator relationship for the future.

The purpose of recognizing your tenured staff is more than making each tenured person feel good. It is about sending a clear message that every person in the school is valued and plays an important role. It tells the community that you value your staff and "we don't just let anyone teach our kids." It bonds and strengthens the relationships within the school. Take the time to make the tenured experience meaningful.

Thank You Day
Make Gratitude a Habit

One of the most important things to teach students is to give thanks when it is deserved. Also, an important academic goal is to improve student writing. We decided to combine Renaissance and writing, and the outcome was the creation of Thank You Day.

Thank You Day is the last Thursday of each month. On that day every student and staffulty member in the school writes a thank you to someone else in the building. The letters can go to other students or staffulty. To keep the focus on writing, the students must use proper letter writing technique. The grade level determines how much the student is asked to write. Some classes base their writing on a picture prompt. At the end of that Thursday, a small group of staffulty organizes the Thank You letters. On Friday morning, the principal delivers the letters to the classrooms for the students and staffulty.

You should see the excitement in the students' eyes as they get letters. It is even a better pick-me-up for the staffulty. You never know how thankful people are for the little things you do.

As the principal, each month on Thank You Day I give a heartfelt thank you to several staff members. I present the thank you in front of their class or group. The staffulty member is extremely happy and posts the thank you in their room.

Thank You Day improves the writing skill of the students, provides recognition to those who deserve it, and best of all, it costs nothing!

This Bud's for You
Thank Each Other with Flowers

This idea is a great way to start a faculty meeting. Prior to the meeting, get some flowers, then have them next to the meeting sign-in sheet. Once everyone arrives and sits down, whoever took a flower can stand up and thank a fellow staff member for whatever they want, then give the flower to the other staff member. This is a feel-good opportunity for the staff to thank each other for the great things they do every day. It publically acknowledges each other and supports positive relationships. Do this at every meeting and you are starting the meeting with positive vibes and warm fuzziness.

Who is the Teacher in the Room?
Remind them that Teachers are People Too

Usually outside each teacher's classroom is the name of the teacher in that room. Why not take that name to the next level? The goal is to highlight the teacher within the room. Whoever walks by the classroom door will be able to relate to the teacher inside because under the teacher's name are credentials and information that highlights the educator. Parents have made connections with teachers because they both went to the same university or they both grew up in the same town. It is a great way to highlight the teacher and help make connections. Some ideas of what to put on the teacher name sign are:

- Identify the level of education the teacher has: BA, BS, MA, DR
- The university or college attended
- Town teacher grew up in
- Photo of the teacher
- Favorite food
- Favorite TV show
- Favorite quote

- Hobby
- Years of teaching
- Year the teacher received Teacher of the Year
- Recognitions

Take It From Me:
Parent Phone Flowchart

Teachers do not get a class on how to talk to parents on the phone. Especially angry parents. It is up to the administration to train the teachers how to talk to parents on the phone and do it well. Teachers must be taught how to navigate the harassing phone call. Below is a flowchart of how to do just that.

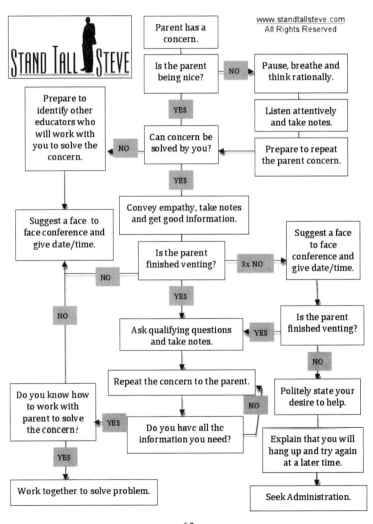

Connecting with Parents and Community

Back to School Night 101
Five Ways to Connect with Parents

I have never outlined specifics for my teachers related to Back-to-School Night. For the most part, I have assumed that everyone knew what to do and did a good job, and I still believe that. Nevertheless, I started to think about our theme "Make It Matter" and how it relates to Back-to-School Night. Back-to-School Night is a reputation builder. It is a time to make a great first impression. When your parents exit the room, you want them sold "hook, line, and sinker" to your teaching style, love of teaching, and methods. This is an opportunity to make "parent relationships" matter. Therefore, here are five things that I think are important in making Back-to-School Night matter.

Shake a Hand: Stand at the door and greet the parents as they enter, similar to how you greet your students at the door when they come to your class. Most of the time teachers hang in the classroom and await the parents. Teachers are a bit nervous and feel secure standing in the classroom. Trust me, by greeting the parents before they enter the room alleviates a lot of that nervous energy. Additionally, it sets a great tone for your time together. Shaking hands and greeting them at the door goes a long way in developing a positive relationship with parents.

Practice: Practice your presentation. In my school the teachers have eight minutes per class period in order to present the material to the parents. Nothing gets you more off track than looking up at the clock and realizing that you only have one minute left and ten more items to go over. At that point you start apologizing to the parents, rushing through your material, blushing, and sounding unprofessional. Take the time to practice the presentation. Don't just review your notes. Stand in front of your room and do the full presentation. If possible, have a colleague watch your presentation and help you get it just right.

Something in Hand: Always offer a handout. The super parent and the mega difficult parent will have a notebook to take notes. Everyone else will most likely scribble information on the back of the schedule they have or do nothing at all. Providing a short half page or full-page handout with your main points on it is very valuable to the parents. It is also beneficial to the parents who are running late, missed most of the presentation, and are now holding you hostage late into the night. Remember to include all of your contact information on each handout you provide. This includes your phone, email, and best time to reach you.

Sign Here... Make sure you have a sign-in sheet for parents or basic information card to fill out. On the sheet or card, have the following:

- Print Name
- Sign Name
- Phone Number
- Email
- Best time to contact

By getting the above information you will have clear evidence of what the parent signature looks like, quick access to their phone numbers, email, and when to call and hold a conversation if needed.

Vocabulary: Be cognizant of the language you use when speaking to parents. Within each industry there is a vocabulary and vernacular that is used. We cannot expect our parents to know all of the words and terminology that we use on a daily basis. Using phrases like, "consistent differentiation through conferencing and instructing within the constructivist method..." does not make you sound smart. Basically, you sound like you are not in touch with the students and a bit of a snob. Use simple everyday language. Slow... it... down. When people are nervous they tend to speed up their talking. Talking fast confuses the parents and leads to them asking questions to clarify what you said. Keep it simple.

Call the School
Make Sure Your Message Reflects Your School's Culture

When parents and community call the main number of the school, what do they hear? It is usually the school secretary saying something like, "...thank you for calling Great Run School. Please listen closely for the following options have changed. Press one for the cafeteria..." It is usually the same message for every school. Nothing differentiates you from any other school or business in the country. Consider updating the message. Instead of having the same message as every other school, here are some ideas for how to personalize your message.

Use Your Students: Find a student who has a great voice and can speak well. Write a script that clearly states what you want people to know when they call. Practice with the students to make sure he/she has it right. When recording the outgoing message with the student, remind the student to smile. You can hear if someone is smiling. It makes the message more pleasant and people are more receptive. Also, if you have an angry parent calling into the school ready to "go off" on a teacher or administrator, hearing a happy child welcome them to the school may help calm them down before speaking to an adult.

Theme and Goals: Start the outgoing message by clearly stating the theme for the school year or a major goal for the school. Doing this clearly outlines what you are about. It does not have to be a long, drawn out statement just a quick mention of what the school is focusing on for the year. It would be even better if the school principal makes the statement.

Slow Down: Nothing is more frustrating than calling a school or business and hearing a voice ramble through the options at lightning speed. Remember, the person calling the school is trying to process what is being said. Think of a time when you listened to a message that was left for you and the person left the phone number as if it were a race, and you had to rewind the message two or three times in order to make sure it is correct. (Come on, I'm not the only one who does that!) The same is true when people call in to the school and listen to the outgoing message. Often they just give up and press "0" for the main office or operator. It's just not worth listening to it again. Whoever leaves the message needs to slow down so callers can process what is being said.

Important Dates: If you are able to change your outgoing message easily, consider providing the dates to important school events. As you know, many parents and community call in order to get clarification on events and times. Cut down on the number of calls by providing the information ahead of time. Remember to change the message once the event is over.

Email Address 2.0
Make the Most of your Email Signature

Take a look at your outgoing email template. Most people have an automatic signature that places your name and basic contact information at the end of every email. Some people get creative and add a motivational quote. This space is actually very valuable real estate. This space is an opportunity to let everyone you email know about something important. Think of your signature space as a place to showcase who you are, what you are doing, and how others can join in. Here are five ways to maximize your signature at the end of an email.

What are you up to? Under your signature, list the dates of important events. If you are a classroom teacher list the dates of the next big project, class trip, or parent visitation. As an administrator list report card dates, concert dates, or PTO meeting times. Update your information every other week. Over time, people will get used to looking for important information at the end of your emails.

The Links: Look for a great article that focuses on parent-child relationships or an article about the importance of schools in the community. Highlight a link under your signature. Not everyone will click the link, but some will. By doing this, you are continually sharing what is important to you and your school.

Color it up! Consider using a different color font within your signature. It doesn't have to be a crazy hot pink. How about a burgundy or navy blue to highlight important information that you want others to know? Please, do not have three or four different colors – that would make it too difficult to read. Just pick one color and possibly bold a word or two that are important.

Contact Me! Don't skimp on providing information about how to get in touch with you. Just because you are sending and receiving an email doesn't mean that is the only way to get back in touch. Within your signature add the following:

- Name
- What do you do in the school?
- Hours that you are available
- Prep time
- School address
- School phone number
- School fax number
- Teacher website (active link)
- School website (active link)
- District website (active link)
- School Facebook page (active link)
- School Twitter name

If you offer all of this information at the end of every email, there is no way a parent can say they didn't know how to get a hold of you or you were not accessible.

Say Cheese! If you are comfortable, consider adding a headshot under your signature. Simply cut and paste a nice, clear image of yourself. Do not use a full body image or a candid photo. You must appear professional and friendly. Also, be sure to shrink the image down to a sensible size. The photo should not be bigger than your typed name. If you don't want to use your photo, consider using the school's mascot. Again, the image should not be bigger than your typed name.

The focus of this idea is to increase communication and improve the image of the school. Through your email signature you can continually share the vision of the school and maximize your public relations opportunities.

I hope you are not planning on adding every idea I shared with you into your email signature. Pick one or two that would work and try it out for a month or two.

Headers and Footers
Don't Waste that Empty Space!

Educators are the kings and queens of paper. We send home papers for a wide variety of reasons – everything from announcement of the field trip to a study guide before the big test. Many are now moving toward using electronic documents in order to "save a tree" or two. Either way, most documents have a header and a footer. A header is the space at the top of the document and the footer is the space at the bottom. These two spaces are golden for the educator. Within this space you can put a wide variety of information that you want to relay to your students or family. For starters, within the footer of EVERY document you send home to parents should have the following:

- Full name
- Contact information
- Best time to contact you or prep times

By providing this information on every document that goes home, you are training your students and parents on how and when to contact you. It will quickly streamline your communication with your parents.

Additional information to place in the header or footer of documents:

- Quote of the week
- Important dates
- Clue to a question
- Classroom website address
- QR code
- School website address
- How to sign up for classroom text
- Extra credit
- Headshot photo
- Mascot image

The goal is to ensure important information is always available all the time on every document that goes home. Your students and parents will start being trained to look to the header or footer for important information. When that time comes that they need to contact you or the school, they can pull out any document from any point throughout the school year and know what to do.

How to Get Ideas!
You Don't have to come up with Everything Yourself

People are always more receptive to ideas they had a hand in suggesting. If you want to know what they are interested in or what their priorities are, ask them!

- At the end of an event, give students a quick paper survey
- Meet with students during lunch once or twice a month
- Send an electronic survey

- Brainstorming session after school
- Post questions on the school's Facebook page
- During lunch ask for a raise of hands if kids liked something or not
- Develop a student advisory group
- Whenever you see a student in the community, just ask!

Leave a Message After the Beep
Make Voicemail More Effective for Everyone

Many teachers now have a phone in their classroom, as well as an extension to call from and to receive messages. In most cases, the teacher's greeting sounds something like this: "This is Mr. Smith's extension. I am not available. Please leave a message after the beep and I will get back to you within 24 hours." That is a typical answer that everyone expects and can be the start of a series of exchanged messages. Look at a voicemail message as an opportunity to share information with whoever is calling, both to provide a better experience for the parent and to save the teacher time and frustration. Consider adding these to a voicemail greeting:

- The room number of the classroom
- The best time to reach you during your prep hour
- The extension of the main office
- The school motto or theme
- Your email address

If possible, record a new message daily or weekly that includes:

- Explanation of the next test or quiz with the day and time
- Homework assignment for the night/week

You can change the message daily, weekly, monthly, or yearly. The goal is to provide information beyond leaving a basic message. Trust me, it goes a long way.

Musical Photos
Give the Paparazzi a Chance

Most schools have a winter and spring concert. The students sing, dance, and perform for parents, family, and friends. The night performances are the best! With over 18 years watching performances as an educator, as well as performing in them since grade school, this is usually what happens:

- The student performers enter the stage getting ready to perform
- Parents stand up and start to wave at their children
- The children can't see them, so the parents start to yell names
- Parents start taking photos from their seats
- Some of the more aggressive parents move towards the stage
- Some bend down as they walk thinking they cannot be seen
- Once near the stage or in the aisle, they start calling for their child to look
- Usually, the parent is very tall and blocks everyone
- Once the concert starts, some parents stay in the aisle or set up a tripod in front of everyone. You are lucky if a fight doesn't break out in the crowd.

Does this sound like your concerts? I have decided to prevent this from happening at concerts by allowing 3-4 minutes for parents to come forward and take photos. The first time I got on the microphone and announced that we will take a couple minutes for photos, you would have thought I'd just given everyone a pound of gold. Parents instantly moved toward the front, waved, called names, and took a bunch of photos without worry. As each minute passed by I announced, "Two minutes left for photos." At the end, everyone respectfully returned to their seats and the concert started.

As each new performance group entered the stage I allowed time for parents to take photos. Yes, the concert was an additional 15 minutes longer. So what? The end result was photos and memories that will last forever.

An additional photo opportunity I started this year was to set up a display in the foyer of the school. I informed the parents that at the end of the performance they could take photos in front of the display in the foyer. I was shocked at how many parents had their children pose with instruments, friends, and me! It made for a wonderful school event.

Note: Make sure you tell the students that there will be 3-4 minutes of photos before they perform. Tell them: look for your parents, smile, and don't complain.

Parent Portrait Night
Help Students and Parents See Each Other

This is an event that I did when I was an art teacher fresh out of college. It is a fun evening event and a great way to develop school and family relationships. The first thing you need to do is talk to your art teacher to make sure he/she is on board and willing to be available for the event. If your art teacher is unable to do it, find a local artist who knows how to teach portraits.

The event is rather clear-cut. Invite parents to return to school at night with their child to draw or paint each other's portrait. Once everyone has arrived, the instructor does a detailed lesson on how to draw portraits. Let the parents and children practice drawing a portrait or two. Once both the parent and child are comfortable to draw a portrait, have the two sit across from each other and start drawing. Have plenty of colored pencils, erasers, or paint available.

Once everyone is finished, display everyone's portrait on the wall for all participants to see. Have some cookies and juice ready.

Everyone take his or her portraits home with a smile.

The focus of this event isn't to make money or bring in tons of people to the school – it is just fun to do. It connects parents and students together and makes the school look great!

Parent Rally
Show Them How It's Done

At the end of each marking period my school has an academic pep rally. This is the time to recognize students and staff for the great work and citizenship they have shown over the quarter. The students go home and tell their parents about the fun they had at the rally and the recognition they got. Why not allow the parents to experience it too? Choose an evening for a rally for parents, and make sure you have volunteers to help. As the parents come in, put them on one of two teams (students are welcome to come with parents.) The parents will participate in fun activities throughout the night, similar to the students during a rally during the day. The recognition of the parents can be both silly and serious, along these lines:

- Didn't have to drop off lunch or homework this year
- Part of the National Honor Society
- Finished the laundry!
- Child was on time to school two weeks in a row
- Went to the gym
- Played the same instrument as their kid
- Ran the vacuum today
- Did a family activity within the past week
- Has served in the military
- Didn't leave dishes in the sink

Photo Op
Provide a School-Themed Background for Photos

Purchase a photo backdrop printed with the school logo on it – easily transportable types are available. Pull it out for special events so students, parents and families can take photos in front of it. This is great for concerts – parents love to take photos of their children after concerts with their instrument. It is also great for recognition ceremonies. For a fun event activity, keep some props in a box so people can make funny faces and dress up, like a photo booth at a party. Don't forget to include them in the yearbook.

Popping In
Parents Appreciate Recognition Too

Fall is the time when many schools have parent/teacher conferences. Here is a neat gesture that will strengthen the relationships between teachers and parents.

Before conferences, go to your local grocery store and get a box of instant popcorn bags. Make sure you have enough for every conference you have. Either print or hand write on labels the following statement: "Thanks for 'popping' in for parent/teacher conferences." You can add additional information like the student's name, your contact information, or a reminder about an upcoming event.

This isn't a huge idea, but a great way to show that extra token of appreciation to the parents. The cost and prep time is minimal and the result is huge. This can also be used for back-to-school night.

Principal Web Page 2.0
Show Your Personality

The focus of the principal's web page is to express your vision for the school and educational philosophy. Additionally, you want the school community to get to know you. Here are some suggestions:

School mission statement: Hopefully, the mission is not a long three-paragraph statement that nobody wants to read. As long as it is short and to the point, put it on the page. Also, a few sentences about how you believe in the mission would be beneficial.

Test scores before you started and test scores now: Consider showcasing test scores that were not as good before you started as principal, and now how much better they are. You can add a few statements about how the staff works hard with the students to get great results. If the scores are not better or the same, I wouldn't suggest posting them.

Basic demographics: Not the demographics of the school, demographics of you! If you are comfortable, share the town you are from, number of kids you have, how long you have been married, years of experience. This information will allow the community to build a relationship with you. If they know you better, they will trust you more.

Favorite quotes: People love positive quotes. Grab a few and post them on your principal's page. Consider a couple of powerful ones and toss in a funny one that everyone knows. Again, this will allow others to get to know you and builds trust.

Favorite educational movies: I tried this one with my monthly newsletter, and I got a huge response from the parents. Some parents sent me emails and others shared how they rented the movies because of my suggestion. Try it and see what happens.

Vision: Share where you see the school going within the next few years. Sharing the vision of the school pulls others into the vision and heart of the school. The more people connected to the vision, the more understanding they will be when decisions are made.

Where is the Principal? Have a section that is updated monthly that shares part of your schedule. Share that you will visit a community soccer game, PTA meeting, BOE meeting, or go white water rafting on the weekend. It shows that you are a professional and normal person – another opportunity to build relationships and make connections.

Photo: You need two photos: one serious and one having fun with kids. I strongly suggest you get them professionally done. Every school has a staff member who loves to take photos and has a great camera. Have that person take some good shots. Don't just have the typical school photo. You need to show some personality.

Link to a great article: As you find great articles about education, post them to your website as a reference. Doing this shares your educational philosophy. Providing a writing of your thoughts on the article is icing on the cake. Not only are you well read, but well written.

Do not include on the website:
- The weather
- Why you made certain decisions
- Information about other schools
- Only data
- The same thing you had last year
- One loooooooonnnnggg paragraph (nobody reads them)

Teacher Trivia
Connect Parents with Teachers via Trivia Games

In the parent newsletter, slip in some trivia about the teachers who work at the school. You can even write an article highlighting specific new teachers in the school. This allows the community and parents to make a connection with the teachers that are in the school. A great twist to this is to send out a text or Tweet to all of the parents with a question about the trivia of the teacher, and the parent who can return that information first or second gets a prize. After doing that a few times you will get parents reading the newsletter more often and the connections become even stronger.

Take It From Me:
Top 6 Ways to Have a
Positive School Culture

1. **Show Respect.** Encourage everyone to be polite and kind to each other. The best way to do that is to do it yourself. Be the model of respect and politeness. Don't talk about negative things. I know, it's easy to focus on bad things that happen in school. It is our natural tendency to focus on negative things; it's often more entertaining. But don't do it! Focus on what is positive and talk about the positive things all the time.

2. **Show Trust.** Mean what you say and follow through with it. Your school environment can become toxic if people cannot trust each other. When distrust is not there, it spreads like wildfire. Soon your school will be branded throughout the community as having a principal who doesn't trust the staff. Make sure you mean what you say and always follow through.

3. **Be Reflective.** Everyone owns the climate of a school. Make sure everyone is involved in the process of reflecting on what works and what does not work. Fix what doesn't work and celebrate what does. The practice of continually reflecting on your work needs to be a habit. Make it a part of your strategic plan. Don't move forward unless you look backwards.

4. **Be Courageous.** Be willing to try new things. I once heard a quote, "Courage isn't the absence of fear, but going on in spite of fear." Schools tend to not take chances, fearing that they will be scrutinized by the community. Thinking things through and taking a chance on something new is the way to improve your school. If the school leader is courageous, takes chances, and tries new things, guess what will happen? That's right; the staff, students, parents, and everyone involved will

feel empowered to do the same.

5. **Be Strategic.** Having a common vision will make all decisions easier to make. Roy Disney stated, "When vision is clear, decisions are easy." He was so right! When you are trying to decide if something is the right thing to do, always refer back to your vision. Does it fit? If it does, go forth and conquer. If it does not, toss it in the trash. Develop an action plan that is clear to understand and follow. Have a clear process of how the organization can get to where it needs to be. The question, "Where are we now?" should never have to be asked. A strategic plan will be clear to everyone and easy to follow.

6. **Be Effective.** How are you spending your time? Are you maximizing the time you have? It may seem that you never have enough time to get everything done. Ask yourself, "What could you do differently?" Make sure everything is working as effectively as possible. Talk with others. Ask for other opinions. Survey your work. Make it a part of your strategic plan. Don"t move forward unless you look backwards.

The Look of the School

Bulletin Board Award
Because Once a Year is Not Enough

If you are in a school with bulletin boards, you know how shabby some boards can be. Additionally, the boards tend to remain the same all year long. A great way to encourage staffuly to spruce them up is to have a monthly or quarterly Bulletin Board Award. Make sure you have groups or individuals assigned to update the bulletin board throughout the year. Select the dates for completion of the boards and the judging. Use the custodial staff as judges – I did this and the custodial staff loved it! They reminded the groups when the boards were due, and made sure the groups got supplies they needed to make the boards great. They asked questions about the reason for the boards and even praised the students who had work on the board or worked on the board. The prize was an announcement to the entire school body and a blue ribbon on the board. At one point, the custodial staff wanted to make the announcement to the school and made a certificate for the winners.

Bulletin Board Themes
Take Your Walls to the Next Level

Most schools have bulletin boards. It is usually up to the principal to determine who decorates what bulletin board when. The concern comes when the boards look bad. Sure, anyone can put some kids' work on a board and call it decorated. Nobody stops to look at it and it does not add to the environment of the school. Here are some ideas to take your boring bulletin boards to the next level.

- **Theme**: Pick a theme for the boards throughout the building for the year or each month. This will allow for a common message to be thread throughout the building.

- **Custodial staff**: Have the custodial staff judge the boards each month. It will increase the influence of the custodial staff.
- **Color theme**: Each month have a color that will be common for all boards.
- **Where's Waldo**: Require that a small school mascot be placed on one or two boards. Tell everyone that they must find it.
- **Beyond the frame**: Don't just decorate within the frame of the board. Extend the decoration beyond the frame to bring interest to the board.
- **Directional signs**: Place directional signs throughout the building pointing to the board.
- **Coalition**: Have questions posted on one board and answers on another board in the building.
- **Coming Soon**: Decorate the board, then cover it with large paper with a "Coming Soon" sign to build anticipation.
- **Share on social media**: Take photos of the boards in the building and post one a week on the school Facebook or other social media pages.
- **Get content from social media**: Post questions on your website or social media sites and provide the answer on a board in the building. This pulls people into the building to get the answer.
- **Quotes**: Provide a bank of positive quotes as a springboard to the decoration of the board.
- **Name**: Name each board a word or character. Whoever is assigned that board must uphold that name with the decoration.
- **Art teacher**: Have your art teacher review the elements of good composition with faculty at the start of the school year to set the expectation for bulletin board design.

Coming Soon!
Build Excitement for Upcoming Attractions

Have you ever driven down the street to see a "Coming Soon" sign in the window of an empty store? Seeing that sign builds curiosity and anticipation for what is to come. As the work starts on the establishment, people take notice and discuss the transformation. Eventually the store hosts a grand opening, and people feel pulled into the store because they have witnessed the growth and creation from empty building to thriving business.

The same concept can be used within your school. If you have a bulletin board or display, simply put a "Coming Soon" sign up before starting to decorate. Leave the sign up there for a day or two. You could put up one or two things to build interest. Have some small sheets of paper on the side and pose the question, "What do you think it will be?" Students and staff will comment and build the buzz. Don't worry; even a bad comment builds anticipation. Have a competition to guess what the final image will be.

The goal is to bring attention to your display. Make sure your display is exciting and interactive. It would be a huge downer to build excitement and a buzz if the final display is boring.

First Impression
It's Never Too Late to Make a Good One

When you walk into the front of your building, what do you see, hear, and smell? In most schools you see a beige wall with a few posters or school projects hung on the wall, and possibly a desk with someone who is checking in people for security reasons. You hear the rush of the traffic outside, a few students in the hallways, or maybe nothing at all. The smell could be many things. You could smell wet carpet from the runner in front of the door, the garbage from the can next to the wall, or the famous aroma of sweaty children.

Any way you look at it, the combination of sights and smells could make anyone entering the building have a less-than-ideal experience. When visitors enter your building, it is the first impression they get of what is important to the school. Don't leave this up to chance. Take a moment, stand outside of your building, walk in the front door, and let your senses take inventory. What is the message your school gives when you enter? Is it a positive first impression? Does your school's culture show in a VTW (Visible, Tangible, Walk-aroundable) way? If the message isn't clear and you are not impressed, here are five ways to change that.

Plug In: If you walk into your building and get a whiff of the last sweaty child that walked by, consider getting a plug-in air freshener. Find an outlet that is close to the front door, get a few fragrant devices, set the strength on low, and enjoy. Having a pleasant smell as you enter the building is a delightful surprise that goes a long way. Make sure you change these monthly.

Boom Box: Purchase a small CD player with speakers and place it near the main entrance. Get a few classical CDs with familiar melodies, set one on repeat, and press play so the music will continue. No need to turn the volume up to 10. Keep it at a level so people can notice the music when they enter. Having calming music playing as people enter helps set the tone. This is especially helpful if you have an angry parent or community member coming in.

Say Cheese: Take several photos of students who attend the school. Pick out a few that are full of energy and have them enlarged to poster size. Frame the photos and arrange them in the lobby. Some people love black and white photos and some like the bright colors. Either way works well. The focus is to showcase what is most important: the students. Having student work on the walls is nice, but how often do you see people stopping to look at it? Displaying beautiful children on the walls will attract more people and make for a positive environment as you enter the school.

Theme: Place a large banner at the main entrance showcasing your theme for the year. This clearly states what is important to everyone who enters. There is no doubt that the school is a positive place for learning.

Paperless: Get rid of all the paper taped to the front door. So often schools tape important messages to the front door. Here is a secret: NOBODY READS THEM! Find another location to post those papers. If you must hang them at the front door, slide them into clear plastic sleeves so they are straight, organized, and not ripped with tape hanging on them. Nothing says total confusion like a school door with ten ripped announcements all over it.

Frame a Mural
Make it Official

I saw this idea at the Jostens Renaissance National Conference. One school had many murals on the walls of the high school. They took some molding and framed many of the murals. Doing this changed the look of the mural – no longer was it a cool mural, but a framed work of art! It was very simple yet extremely powerful. First, make sure your school has murals. Once you have murals, look to see which ones could benefit from a frame. It may surprise you how good they will look.

High Five Wall
Let Them Bounce off the Walls – With Purpose

A great way to start a tradition with your new incoming students is for them to leave a positive mark on the school. During your new student orientation have each student paint their hand and place the handprint on a designated wall. Have the students use a Sharpie marker to write their name under the handprint. Above the handprints paint a quote or the year of the class. Leave the handprints on the wall until that class leaves/graduates from the school. Before leaving the school or walking out to graduation, have the students walk past the wall. I guarantee that each student will look for their hand and place their hand over it. It will be an emotion-filled moment for each student.

As new students enter the class, make sure they get an opportunity to add their hand to the wall. As students leave the class, leave their hand up. It is a great remembrance for those who were with them throughout the years.

Most Amazing Locker Contest
Give Them a Reason to Keep it Neat

If you've never seen a middle school locker, just imagine a bottomless pit of despair. At the end of the school year we would find all kinds of foul items. In an effort to make this better, we hosted the "Most Amazing Locker Contest." We set a date for judging and the only rule was that nothing living could be in the locker. Otherwise, they could decorate them however they wanted and we even offered a day after school when they could stay to decorate. Each student who wanted to participate taped a form on the front of the locker. After each locker was judged, a certificate was placed on the inside and a thank you note posted on the front. The winning locker was announced and photos were posted on the in-house television station and on a designated bulletin board.

The following year we ramped it up by getting a sponsorship from The Container Store. The Container Store donated some organizational items and a ribbon for the winner. It is amazing how fancy the lockers were. We had chandeliers years before they were popular. We had everything from disco balls to shag carpeting to wallpaper.

Over the Top!
Make Visitors Say, "Wow"

Sometimes it is okay to go "Over the Top" within the school. What do I mean by Over the Top? Over the Top means an event or visual representation that is beyond what others would think is possible within your school. The Over the Top item may be connected to spirit week, charitable event, military, or just because.

The goal is to make people say, "Wow!" when they see it or experience it. The Over the Top event will not be easy to do. You will have to get the support of others and possibly put out some money. You may have to work on it throughout the year.

Why have an Over the Top event? An Over the Top event is an opportunity for the school to send a major message to the entire community what is important to you. It expresses how you work together, the values, the mission, and the vision of the school. Providing media coverage not only shares the vision with the community but solidifies the school's relationship with the media. Yes, the focus of the school is learning, but having an Over the Top experience provides a different kind of learning that goes beyond the curriculum.

In my school the guidance counselors had every student sign a hand cutout. Signing the hand signifies the student will lend a hand to prevent violence and keep the peace. First they die cut over 900 hands. The guidance counselors visited every student during lunch periods to have them sign and collect the hands. (900+ students) They took the many hands and created a huge 8-foot tall peace sign. We took the peace sign and hung it within the stairwell. Everyone who sees it for the first time says one word: WOW!

Restroom Signs
Make Every Part of the School Positive

Organize a group of students who are artistic and positive. Work with the students on finding quotes and sayings that are inspiring to them, and have conversations about whether these are appropriate and inspiring to others. In the ladies' room you might use, "You Look Great!" "You Can Do It!" or "Who Cares What They Say!" In the boys' room: "You Got This!" "You Da Man!" or "You Got Game!" Ask them to paint the quotes on the walls of the restrooms to completely change the environment. Use bright colors and bold letters so the messages can be seen. If you are unable to paint in the restrooms, make some signs and have them laminated. Be sure to use strong tape so they stay up.

School Theme T-shirt 2.0
Honor Each Year and its Theme

Having a theme for the entire school is a great way to focus everyone's efforts toward a common goal. The best themes are those that are motivational, results driven, and fun to say. Having a theme that is a play on words allows it to be said more often and used in conversation.

Now the question is: what are you going to do with the theme now that you have it? You need to maximize the use of the theme. When students, staff, and community enter your building, do they instantly know what the theme is? Consider placing a large banner in the front of your school or the front foyer of the school. Try to make the banner larger than life. Doing this sends a clear message of what you are about, and it is a continual reminder of what is important at your school.

T-shirts are walking billboards and are key parts of VTW. Give theme T-shirts out to your staff. Have them wear the shirts on the first day of school. Having all the adults in the school wear the theme T-shirts on the first day takes the pressure off of them to pick an outfit for the first day of school, shows unity throughout the staff, and sends a clear message about what is important at your school.

Have some theme T-shirts available to the students as well. You can sell the shirts for profit or give them away as recognition. Throughout the year have theme days when everyone wears the theme T-shirts. At the end of the year final rally, retire the theme. Talk to the creative people in the school and have them develop a small ceremony to retire the theme for the year. At the end of the ceremony, frame the T-shirt and hang it in the hallway, move the larger banner to another part of the school, or make a smaller banner to hang in the gym, media center, hallway, or cafeteria. Basically, find a way to show respect to the theme that supported the school throughout the year.

See the Signs
The Writing is on the Wall – In a Good Way!

Look around your school. What messages are people seeing? I'm not speaking metaphorically. What are the actual written signs within your school? Many schools have the pre-made banners that you can get from a catalog. I agree, some of the banners are very good and share a quality message. Nevertheless, I feel it to be important to showcase written signs that are specific to the vision, culture, and mission of your school. Additionally, think creatively about where the signs will be displayed:

- Door windows
- Floor
- Steps
- Food trays
- Back of chairs
- Mirrors
- Inside every locker
- Parking spots
- Marquee
- School letterhead

Think carefully about what words you will use. Don't use too many quotes or statements. Stick with a few that drive home the mission and vision of the school. Repeat the quotes and statements often. The goal is to purposefully encourage the school community to embrace the vision of the school.

Sidewalk Chalk
Welcome Students Back with Color

This idea is simple yet powerful. Use sidewalk chalk to welcome students and staff for the first day of school. On the walkway leading to the main entrance and other doors to the school, write words of encouragement to welcome everyone to the start of school. If you are not excited about sitting on the ground and drawing in chalk, reach out to school and community groups to do the work:

- Boy Scouts/Girl Scouts
- Local church
- Honor Society
- Student government
- Local summer camp
- PTO/PTA

Be very specific about what you want to say. Give a list of words or statements that would send the message that you want, such as:

- "Welcome Back!"
- School theme
- School pride statements
- Mascot image
- Color parking spots
- Arrows pointing toward the door
- Instructions for students/staff
- Schedule of events
- Name of staff

Consider the colors you want to use. Would you like a rainbow of colors? Should certain colors go in front of certain doors? Should all the colors be the same? Be sure to take a few pictures for the yearbook.

The focus is to celebrate the start of the school year. You can be as simple or as elaborate as you like. A little bit of chalk goes a long way.

Star Table
Who has the Cleanest Table in the Lunchroom?

I started to notice that the lunchroom tables were a hot mess. There was food on the floor, the table tops were not wiped down, and the kids really didn't care. I could see the frustration from the custodian every day. Therefore, we came up with Star Table. Star Table is when the lunchroom supervisors pick the best table at the end of the week, and we had a chart on the wall to keep track. If a table got the weekly Star Table two times, they would be identified officially as Star Table. That table would receive an official table top flag to keep at the table for the week and they would be called up first for lunch. Additionally, we would announce the winner of the Star Table award over the announcements at the end of the day.

Magic started to happen. The students started cleaning the table tops and underneath as best they could. We went out and purchased brooms and dustpans for them and they took to it right away. The custodian was extra excited because it was less that he had to do and the students started to take pride in their areas. I could honestly say we had the cleanest cafeteria in the tri-state area.

Theme Stairs
Make Going Upstairs Fun!

I saw a photo online of a house with positive quotes about the family written on the vertical part of their stairwell. A light bulb went off in my head: I had a large center stairwell in my school. I had the themes we used over the years made into rub-on stickers, and then put them onto the vertical part of the stairwell. It was great to see a reminder of the history of the school in such a well-traveled location. Other options could include:

- Multiplication facts
- Addition facts

- Positive quotes
- Colors
- Names of historical figures
- Class of _____
- Mascot
- Team names

Where Are You Going?
Encouraging Seniors to Share Their College Plans

After attending our first Jostens Renaissance meeting, we were immediately hooked and started making plans to implement ideas in our building. This idea revolved around our graduating class of seniors. Using one of the large bulletin boards near our cafeteria, a natural gathering place for students, we highlighted where our seniors were headed for the following school year. We titled it "Seniors, Where Are You Going?" and designed the bulletin board to look like a road or track. Then, we created various colors of die-cut cars and passed them out to our soon-to-be graduates.

On the cars, we asked each senior to write his or her name and college or education plans for the following year. We placed the cars on the roadway bulletin board so the underclassmen could get a real idea of their friends' goals and, hopefully, inspire them to consider where their education might lead.

Based on the information submitted by the seniors, we then made a list of all the places the students planned to go the following year. During the last week of school for seniors, we hosted a spirit week competition where one of the daily themes was to dress in your future college attire. Over the PA system, the principal asked all seniors to stand up in their classes while he congratulated them and read the list of colleges, trade schools, universities, etc.

This was a no-cost way to recognize that many of our seniors were headed to college the following school year and a way to announce their plans. Our seniors loved showing off what four years of hard work in high school was allowing them to do the next school year.

WOW Committee
Unleash Your School's Interior Designers

The WOW committee is a fun name for an interior decorating committee. Go out and recruit the teachers or students who have an eye for interior decorating or artistic flair. Meet together and start looking around the building for locations that do not look WOW. Basically, identify the locations in the school that do not seem very impressive. A good place to start is the main entrance. If possible, give the committee a small budget to work with and allow them to start decorating that area. You'll be surprised what they will come up with and do. It will completely change the look and the feel of your school. Allow the committee to decorate seasonally. Once the committee has decorated one area, allow them to continue to decorate other areas around the school. The end result is a beautiful school that others take pride in. Another option would be to allow the committee to go into classrooms and decorate them for teachers if they so choose. The goal is for people to walk around your school and say WOW!

Take It From Me: It's Up 2 U

I was in ninth grade. The basketball game just started and I was feeling good about how I was going to do throughout the game. As the game went on, it was clear that my head was not in the game and I was making too many little mistakes – not talking enough to my teammates, not using my left hand for a left layup, doing a fast break even though there were three defenders right next to me. What was I thinking?

After some time the coach called a timeout. He pulled everyone over and pointed right in my face. He very forcefully outlined all of my mistakes. Going back into the game I had a bad attitude. My performance didn't get any better, but worse. Even though I was trying to do the right thing, I couldn't get over how the coach yelled at me like that. How dare he put his finger in my face!

Just before halftime, the coach pulled me out of the game. I jogged over to him with my head tilted waiting to hear what he had to say. He told me to have a seat on the bench until my attitude changed and I start acting like I want to play basketball. I grumbled a "whatever" and sat down at the end of the bench. As I sat down I mentally checked out of the game. I didn't play for the remainder of the game.

Everything we do is a choice. It is a choice if we try or give up, learn or get by, exist or live. No matter what we choose to do, we must live with the consequences of our actions. What would you do? Seriously! Be honest with yourself. When you get offended, do you try to look up and be positive, or do you concentrate on the offense and never get the problem resolved? Either way you have to live with the consequences of your choice. It is not easy to move past an offence and see the silver lining. Sometimes you may feel that you must make a stand simply for the principle of the situation. Either way, It's Up 2 U, the choice is yours.

We can argue about how the coach spoke to me and the other players. He could have had a different approach to bring out the best in the players. Nevertheless, I had a choice. Either I could get a bad attitude, stand my ground on principle, and eventually not play; or take it for what it is worth and make the best out of it and finish the game. On the bus ride home from the game, the coach called me to the front and asked me to sit with him. We talked about how I responded to him during the game and what other options there were. He explained that when I was told to sit on the bench until I had a better attitude, I could have sat right next to him right away and said, "I'm ready, coach."

Not everything is going to go your way. The ideas that you try to implement may not work. Others will try to offend you. You can either let it get to you or stand tall and keep it moving. It's Up 2 U!

Index